NEW BEGINNINGS

A CREATIVE WRITING GUIDE FOR WOMEN WHO HAVE LEFT ABUSIVE PARTNERS

SHARON DOANE, M.S.W.

SEAL PRESS

To my parents, Eileen and Allan Doane,
for their unwavering love and support

Seal Press
3131 Western Avenue, Suite 410
Seattle, Washington 98121
Email: sealprss@scn.org

Library of Congress Cataloging-in-Publication Data
Doane, Sharon.
New beginnings : a creative writing guide for women who have left abusive partners / Sharon Doane.
(New leaf series)
1. Abused women—United States—Psychology. 2. Abused women—Rehabilitation—United States. 3. Creative writing. I. Title.
HV6626.2.D63 1996 362.82'924—dc20 96–13790
ISBN 1-878067-78-8

Printed in the United States of America
First printing, May 1996
10 9 8 7 6 5 4 3 2 1

Distributed to the trade by Publishers Group West
In Canada: Publishers Group West Canada, Toronto, Canada
In Europe and the U.K.: Airlift Book Company, London, England

Cover and text design by Clare Conrad

Acknowledgments

I would like to extend my gratitude to the many women who passed through the doors of the Family Shelter during my time there, and who impressed me with their strength, resiliency and courage. Likewise, I would like to thank my colleagues in the domestic violence field, with special appreciation to Mary R., with whom I struggled and grew.

I am especially indebted to the women who donated their writing to this book because they wanted to help other women who have left abusive partners by sharing their stories and experiences. Confidentiality prevents me from thanking them by name, but each of them has my respect and gratitude.

I would also like to thank my editor, Faith Conlon, who helped give the book shape and clarity, as well as Holly Morris, also of Seal Press, who nurtured the project along in its initial stages.

Most importantly, I would like to thank my husband, Juan Morquecho, for his unflagging belief in me and whose support helped make the writing of this book possible.

Contents

What This Book Is About and How to Use It 3
Four Women's Stories: Graciela, Alicia, Maggie and Anna 9

Part I: Finding Safety: Identifying What You Need to Be Physically and Emotionally Safe

1 "Am I in Danger Now?" 19
2 Feeling Safe 23
3 "I Feel Vulnerable When. . . " 27
4 Having a Safety Plan 31
5 "My Ex Keeps Doing It: How I Can Protect Myself" 34
6 "Someone I Thought I Could Count On Who Disappointed Me" 39
7 "Someone Who Came Through for Me When I Needed Them" 43
8 "What Might Lure Me Back" 46
9 Learning to Say No 50

Part II: What Happened: Remembering, Grieving, Letting Go

10 "Why I Left" 57
11 The Last Straw 60
12 "Why I Stayed" 64
13 "I'm Not Crazy—There Were Good Times, Too" 67
14 "What My Life Would Be Like If I Hadn't Left" 70
15 A Letter to Your Abuser 73
16 A Letter to Someone Significant in Your Life About What Happened 76
17 Letting Go 79
18 "What I Like Best About My New Life" 82

Part III: Moving On: Finding Out What You Really Want for Yourself

Section I: Healthy Relationships

19 The Difference Between Being Lonely and Being Alone 89
20 Caring or Controlling? 93
21 The Difference Between Being Taken Care Of and Being Supported 96
22 Sex and Intimacy 99
23 "What I Want in a Relationship" 102

Section II: Focusing on Yourself

24 "What I Want for Myself" 107
25 Remembering and Reclaiming Childhood Goals 109
26 "I'm Most Proud Of. . . " 113
27 "Making My Own Choices" 115
28 Finding Support and Making New Friends 118
29 "What Success Means to Me" 122
30 Setting Goals—and Achieving Them 125
31 Taking Care: Eating, Exercising, Relaxing 129
32 Meditation and Creative Visualization 132

Suggested Resources and Reading 135

NEW BEGINNINGS

What This Book Is About and How to Use It

Have you left a relationship where your partner:

- Called you names?
- Said demeaning things about you?
- Kept you from seeing friends or family members?
- Was excessively possessive or jealous and regularly accused you of flirting or having affairs when you weren't?
- Made you account for every minute of your time?
- Controlled the money, even what you earned?
- Threw or destroyed objects, such as the phone, when angry?
- Slapped, shoved, hit, punched, kicked, bit, burned or otherwise hurt you?
- Forced you to have sex when you didn't want to or in ways you didn't want?
- Justified "punishing" you because he says the Bible (or

other sacred book) said a wife is to be obedient to her husband?
- Threatened or attacked you with a weapon?
- Threatened to disappear with your children if you left him?
- Threatened to kill you or himself if you left him?

If you answered yes to any of these questions, chances are your partner was someone who abused power and control and, as part of that, abused you. This may come as a surprise to you. Many women whose partners are controlling or violent don't think of themselves as being in an abusive relationship. This is especially so for women whose partners are emotionally but not physically violent. Such women often say, "But he doesn't *hit* me."

It's easy to understand why some women do not want to define themselves as abused. Many people still have the misconception that women who are abused by their partners are weak and passive, perhaps even masochistic or stupid. Some people, professionals included, ask, "Why doesn't she just leave?" This question suggests that there is a simple, safe solution to a complex, often dangerous situation; it also implies that the problem lies within the woman, and not with her abusive partner.

The fact is, many women do leave abusive partners. They leave with the help of shelters, social workers, law enforcement, friends, family or on their own. They set up new lives as single women and single parents. They get jobs, go back to school and utilize social services to help them get back on their feet. Women who endure and survive abusive relationships often have a great deal of strength, courage and creativity.

Being on your own after an abusive relationship is not

always easy. Continued harassment by your ex-partner, economic problems, single parenthood and loneliness are just a few of the difficulties you may be facing. Add them all up and you've got a lot of stress. Life may sometimes seem so overwhelming and hard that you think about going back to your ex, hoping he will have changed. Besides, you miss him; perhaps you still love him.

After you leave an abusive relationship, you need support in order to face the challenges of your new life, just as you needed support to break free from the relationship in the first place. That's where this book comes in. *New Beginnings* will help you clarify what really happened in your relationship and how you can feel safe and supported in your new life. It will also help you identify what you want for yourself as you begin this challenging and exciting part of your life. You can use this book on your own, as part of a formal or informal support group or with a counselor or therapist. If there is a support group in your community for women who have been abused, consider checking it out. You can learn a lot from other women who have dealt with what you are dealing with, and their support can help you, especially when you're feeling low. To find such a group, try calling your local domestic violence hotline or an organization such as the YWCA.

Remember that starting a new beginning is a process and, like any process, there will be times when you take one step forward, two steps back. This is normal. Keep faith that you are strong enough, smart enough and have enough inner resources to accomplish your goals and attain the kind of life you want.

Although *New Beginnings* is designed for women who have left abusive partners, much of the book can also be utilized by any woman who feels that something was unhealthy in one or more of her past relationships. *New Beginnings* will help you put a name to whatever happened in relationships that made you feel uncomfortable or uneasy and identify what you do and do not want in a new relationship as well as in other aspects of your life.

New Beginnings is divided into three parts: "Finding Safety: Identifying What You Need to Be Physically and Emotionally Safe," "What Happened: Remembering, Grieving, Letting Go" and "Moving On: Finding Out What You Really Want for Yourself." You may want to read straight through the book or you may choose to skip around. You also may want to return to certain chapters at different times. The last part of the book is especially useful for any woman who wishes to sort out her goals, dreams and aspirations so that she can begin taking steps to achieve them.

Although some abusers are women, in either lesbian or heterosexual relationships, the majority of perpetrators are men and the majority of victims are women. As such, *New Beginnings* uses this model and is addressed to women who have had abusive male partners.

Your Turn to Write

New Beginnings gives you the chance to write your own story through the use of creative writing exercises. These exercises are designed to help you express what you think and how you feel about various aspects of your experience. The guidelines which accompany each exercise are suggestions only—you can approach the writings any way you want; there is no right or wrong method. You can make a list, write a letter, create a poem or compose a journal entry. *This is your story and you have the right to tell it the way you want.*

General Guidelines for All the Writings

You may be an experienced writer or this may be your first try at writing. Regardless, you may feel intimidated by the blank page and wonder where to start.

In school we get the message that the only good writing is very formal, with perfect spelling, punctuation and grammar. In our anxiety to write well, we get overly focused on the mechanics, and creativity gets lost. In the end, our efforts are like hothouse tomatoes—perfectly shaped and colored, but totally tasteless.

To overcome the stilted quality of "hothouse" writing, try to write the way you speak. Think how easily you tell a story about something that happened to you when you're on the phone with a friend. You describe the event in dramatic detail. The story flows effortlessly, you don't constantly pause, wondering what to say next. But if you try to *write* the same story, you may freeze up. Your internal censor, who perhaps has the voice of your sixth grade teacher, starts criticizing your work. Pretty soon you get frustrated and put the piece away, unfinished.

The writing exercises in this book are not geared toward creating polished pieces of writing that would please your sixth grade teacher. The exercises are designed to help you identify feelings and give clarity and coherence to your experiences. Don't worry about grammar, punctuation and spelling. Don't compare your work to the writings by other women in this book; each individual woman's story is different and all are equally valid.

You might find it easiest to write from your heart if you

give yourself a time limit, such as ten to twenty minutes, when working on a piece. This will help you bypass your internal censor—you simply won't have the time to dwell on what you're going to write or whether it will be any good. Just write. Try to write without stopping and without lifting your pen from the paper. If you get stuck, write "I'm stuck" or "what's next?" over and over until the words that express your inner feelings come out. However, if another method works better for you, by all means, use it.

This book may call up many painful or frightening feelings. Each time you plan to read it, try to be in a place where you feel safe and where you won't be interrupted. Wait until the kids are in bed or in school. Think of a supportive person you can call if you start feeling overwhelmed. You might find it helpful to work on the book for only an hour at a time—reading, thinking, feeling, writing—and then putting it back on the shelf, safely contained until you're ready to work on it again. Go slowly and be gentle with yourself. Remember: you do have the strength and courage to undertake this journey.

Four Women's Stories: Graciela, Alicia, Maggie and Anna

Any woman of any age, race, class, religion or ethnic group can find herself in a relationship with an abusive partner. Throughout this book you will read writings by women who have left abusive male partners. All of their words are authentic, but identifying information such as names, ages, occupations and characteristics of children have been changed for reasons of safety and confidentiality. Each woman's story found below is a composite of the stories of hundreds of women who have been abused with whom I have had the privilege to work. These stories do not represent the lives of all women who have been abused, but you will probably recognize some of your own experiences in them.

. . .

Graciela

Graciela is a thirty-three-year-old Latina who lives with her seven-year-old daughter, Carmen. Graciela has been on her own for two years now. Before that she spent nine years in an on-again, off-again relationship with Hector, who is Carmen's father. Graciela met Hector when they were both residents at an alcohol rehabilitation center. In groups at the facility, Hector seemed charming and deeply committed to staying sober. Although a string of bad relationships had made her leery of men, Graciela found herself falling for Hector, who showered her with attention.

When they left the rehab, Hector moved in with Graciela. Graciela wanted to pursue a career as a journalist and enrolled in a program at the community college. She was surprised to find Hector unsupportive of her efforts. He was unhappy about the time she devoted to her studies and accused her of having a boyfriend at school. Whenever Graciela showed him her stories, he told her that they were no good and that she had no talent. One evening when she returned half an hour late, Hector refused to let her into the apartment. She stood in the hallway, bewildered, as he screamed and threw things behind the locked door. It was not long after that that he hit her for the first time. Graciela decided that maybe she had been neglecting Hector and that she was being selfish to spend so much time on her studies.

Hector started drinking again and Graciela was terrified that she would lose her own sobriety. In the face of Hector's drinking and his violence, Graciela decided she had to leave him. That was her first time at a domestic violence shelter. Hector got word to her that he would kill himself if she didn't come back. He told her he loved her and couldn't live without her. Overcome by guilt, Graciela returned home. She did not go back to school.

Graciela and Hector got married when Graciela got pregnant several years later. Once Carmen was born, Graciela felt she now had practically no chance of leaving Hector. Hector's constant physical, sexual and emotional abuse made Graciela feel as if she were losing her mind. Through it all, however, she stayed sober.

Graciela left and returned to Hector four times before making the final break. She utilized a carefully built support system of shelter counselors, women she met at a group run by the shelter and friends from Alcoholics Anonymous to help her set up a new life for herself and Carmen. She is divorced from Hector now, although she still has contact with him because of his court-ordered visitation with Carmen. The last two years have not been easy—Hector continues to harass her. Graciela has been working hard to rebuild her self-confidence and self-esteem and has returned to school to pursue her dream of becoming a journalist. Recently she sold her first story to the local newspaper, and hopes this is the beginning of a successful career.

Alicia

Alicia is a twenty-six-year-old white woman who lives with her children, Sandra, Michael and Linda. Alicia met Jeff at a church function when she was eighteen. They were married within a year and the children followed soon after. Alicia was a good student and had planned to go to college. Before they were married, Jeff enthusiastically supported her plans, but when she became pregnant he insisted that she stay home. It was while she was pregnant that Jeff hit her for the first time.

Alicia spent seven years with Jeff, during which time she never told anyone about his beatings or how he constantly criticized her. To make matters worse for Alicia, memories of being sexually abused as a child started surfacing. Jeff would not allow her to seek counseling.

Alicia left Jeff when she realized that his violent behavior was adversely affecting the children. She went to her parents' house only to have them urge her to return to her husband. But Alicia persevered, found an apartment in a different area, got a job as a receptionist and enrolled in evening classes at the local college where she was given a scholarship.

Alicia admits that making the break has not been easy. Her parents continue to invite Jeff to family gatherings. Because she and Jeff owned a small business together, there are times when she must see him regarding business matters. When he's alone with her, Jeff drops his nice-guy facade and makes derogatory comments. He constantly threatens to fight her for custody of their children—which is Alicia's biggest fear.

Still, Alicia says she feels a tremendous sense of relief and freedom being away from Jeff. Her school success reminded her that she is an intelligent woman, something she'd lost sight of during her years with Jeff. Alicia has built up a network of friends from whom she gets the emotional support her parents are unable to provide. She has started seeing a therapist to work through her childhood experience of abuse and has begun helping to educate the public about domestic violence through the local shelter. Next year she will graduate from college with a degree in psychology and hopes to find a job working with children and families.

. . .

Maggie

Maggie is a forty-two-year-old African-American woman who lives on her own with her two children, Meagan, twelve, and Robert, fourteen. Maggie had been married to the children's father for ten years when he died of cancer. Maggie was devastated but used her natural resourcefulness to learn how to manage as a single mother. When Maggie met Russell, she was working as a home health aide and had just received her general equivalency diploma (GED). Her goal was to return to school and become a nurse.

Russell told her he'd had a hard life growing up, going from one foster home to another after being abandoned by his parents. He had fathered a son by a woman in a different state and he said he felt heartbroken because he never got to see the boy. Maggie felt sorry for Russell and helped him out by lending him money and letting him use her telephone and address to receive messages and mail. Soon, he had moved in.

Maggie describes her six-month relationship with Russell as short but intense. Looking back, she believes he manipulated her into thinking they had the romance of the century. They had gotten together when Maggie was feeling vulnerable and lonely after her husband's death, and Russell, who initially was very attentive, seemed to be the answer to her prayers.

Russell did not physically abuse Maggie but the threat was always there. He often flew into rages and smashed things around the house. He also used psychological violence, which included constant criticism. Maggie was especially hurt by his cruel remarks about her parenting; she had always prided herself on being a good mother to Meagan and Robert. Maggie began to understand how dangerous Russell's behavior was when he smashed a vase and a piece of flying glass cut Robert.

Maggie questions her decision to leave Russell because she still loves him. "If it weren't for the kids, I might be back with him," she says. Each day she strengthens her resolve to stay away from him by renewing her commitment to a safe, healthy life for herself and her children. She focuses on her goal of becoming a nurse and hopes to be enrolled in a nursing program within the next two years.

Anna

Anna is a nineteen-year-old white woman who lives with her twin toddlers, Josh and Ashley. Anna grew up in the rural Midwest. She and Bill met in high school; when Anna got pregnant they both dropped out and moved into a small trailer together. Bill got a job as a stockboy at the liquor store and they managed to scrape by.

Bill had always been controlling in their relationship—he told Anna what to wear and who her friends could be—and he also began hitting her as the pregnancy progressed. Anna describes how her excitement over the news that she was carrying twins turned to horror when Bill responded by punching her in the stomach.

Anna says she put up with Bill's battering because she didn't want to be a teenage single mother. Also, violence from male partners wasn't new to her: her father had hit her mother and both of her older sisters were involved with abusive men. Although she didn't like it, Anna thought that was just how relationships were.

When Anna ended up in the hospital emergency room after a severe beating by Bill, a social worker told her about the local battered-women's shelter. For the first time Anna realized she was not alone and that there were alternatives to staying with an abusive man. She and her children went to the shelter. During their stay, Bill was arrested for stealing from the store where he worked and ended up in jail. Anna and the children relocated and started a new life. At first, Anna found life on her own with two babies too difficult; she felt scared and alone. After Bill was released from jail she returned to him twice before making a final break.

Anna is working hard to identify what she wants for herself, something she never had the opportunity to do before. Although sometimes her life is stressful—there's never enough money and the twins take up a lot of time and energy—Anna says she feels stronger and more clear-headed than ever before. She concentrates on learning how to take care of the twins and herself, plans to get her GED and is considering a career in sales.

PART I

Finding Safety: Identifying What You Need to Be Physically and Emotionally Safe

1 "*Am I in Danger Now?*"

Good question, isn't it? It's probably one you became familiar with when you lived with your abuser. Part of you was always on alert, constantly checking for those signals that indicated he was about to blow. You gauged his mood by the way he slammed the car door, or how he looked at you when he came home from work. In a split second, you could tell if you were safe—or not. You were probably very good at detecting these signs because you're a survivor.

But what about now? You've left him, but unfortunately that doesn't mean you're completely safe from his violence. Some abusers stalk their former wives or girlfriends, with the intention of harming them or even killing them. This information is not presented to frighten you, but rather to validate your concerns about your former partner's potential violence now that you have left. Having concerns does not mean you shouldn't have left! After all, what would have happened to you if you had stayed? And aren't the children better off in a home without violence?

Anna says there is no easy answer to the question of whether she is in danger from Bill now. In addition to fearing for her physical safety, Anna is also concerned about the dangers to her emotional well-being. Her poem describes how hard it is to feel completely safe and secure from a former abuser, yet it also expresses the hope that she can successfully move on.

Am I in Danger Now?

Am I in danger now?
I couldn't really say—
I'd like to say yes
But I really don't know.
He doesn't know exactly where I live
But he does know what town.
I feel safer when he doesn't know where.
My physical being is safe—
        I believe
But what about my emotional being?
I don't get nauseated talking on the phone
But in the same room I get queasy
And look for a way out.
Today I can tell him
What I don't want to talk with him about—
What is none of his business to know—
How our kids are doing,
How I am doing.
I still feel obligated to answer his questions.

Today when he says can we get back
        together

I asked have you changed
Did you give up drinking and drugs?
When he answers no
I tell him I don't think so. It would only be a superficial
external change.

But even if he had. . .
I believe I wouldn't
Things have changed so much
No, I have changed so much.
I remember the emotional pain—
the loneliness, the fear, the darkness, the despair,
the emptiness, the anger, the shame,
the degradation, the heartache,
the crying, the sadness.

And I remember
So when I'm asked
Am I in danger now?
There is no easy answer.
But I remember
and hopefully I learn
and go on from there.

Your Turn to Write: "Am I in Danger Now?"

Now that you're on your own, you mustn't forget to use your instincts about potential danger. You can begin by assessing what may be dangerous in your current life.

Take a moment and carefully consider your situation. It

is very important to be honest with yourself, because you will need to take steps to deal with potential danger if you are not safe. You know your ex better than anyone else does, so trust your instincts if you feel there's something to be afraid of.

You might want to start by making a list of some of the most dangerous events in your relationship. Did he threaten you with a weapon? Did he drive recklessly with you in the car? Did he force you to take drugs or alcohol? Write down how you felt when those things happened. Is there anything happening in your current life that gives you the same frightened feeling? Write down these things and how they make you feel.

If you do identify danger while doing this exercise, you may want to call your local domestic violence hotline to discuss your options with a counselor. If the threat is more imminent, call the police.

2 Feeling Safe

When was the last time you truly felt safe? For women who have gone through years or months of abuse, it may be difficult to remember what *safe* actually feels like. Perhaps you have never lived on your own before. The prospect of doing that now may be frightening, especially if your abuser has told you time and again that you must rely on him for protection.

Many abusers count on their ex-partners' fears to keep them feeling vulnerable; they manipulate their ex-partners' emotions, hoping to get them to come back by cracking their defenses. Graciela told of how she called Hector during their second separation, after she received a series of late-night obscene phone calls. Later, after he had moved back in and the violence had flared up again, she realized it was probably Hector who had made those calls.

Alicia had been on her own for six months when she

wrote the following poem. A survivor of childhood incest, Alicia found that her husband's repeated sexual abuse opened up old scars and made night a particularly terrifying time. In her poem, "Safe at Night," she looks back at her childhood abuse and the fear she experienced while living with her husband, contrasting those situations against the joy she finds in her present life.

Safe at Night

Locked doors
Pulled-down blinds
Knife under my bed
Ready, on hand, for whatever demons come
My way.

Chains on the doors
Phone by the bed
Yet all those physical traps
Don't keep the demons away
That are lurking in my head.

I find it odd
That I didn't lock the doors at night
I didn't have chains and bolts
On the doors when I was with him.

I was sleeping with my terror
And making him dinner every night.

I find it odd
That I never slept with a knife
Under my bed
Until I remembered when
My grandfather abused me.

Safe at night
Now means
Facing the demons in my head.
I use a sword of steel blue
Power
My mind
And my friends cheering
Me on.

I stand straight and tall
Not ducking and cringing.

Safe at night
Now means
Having time to myself
Time to help myself
Think and grow
To feel my own power.

Safe at night
Now means
Finding the joy and beauty
In myself
Not being afraid of
What I will find.

Safe at night
Now means
Free from the
Fear
Of being myself.

Your Turn to Write: Feeling Safe

In this exercise, write about feeling safe. What does safe mean to you and how does it (or might it) feel? What do you need in order to feel safe? What keeps you from feeling safe? Consider external factors: does your ex-partner drive by the house at all hours of the day and night? Do you live in an unsafe neighborhood with a high crime rate? Is your home in an isolated area? Has your ex threatened to come to the house? Think about internal factors that keep you from feeling safe. Do you give yourself messages such as "It really isn't safe for a woman to live alone" or "There's really no way I can protect myself from him"?

Write down ways in which to make yourself feel safer. If your ex is harassing you, perhaps it would make you feel safer to have a current court order of protection against him. What about informing people, such as your neighbors, your landlord and the police, about what your ex is doing, and asking for their support? If you live in an isolated or crime-ridden location, consider moving.

Write down how you can overcome the internal obstacles that keep you from feeling safe. Try replacing negative messages with positive ones, such as "Lots of women live safely on their own and I can, too," "There are many ways I can protect myself from him and I'm going to learn and utilize every one of them," and "I deserve to be and feel safe."

3 *"I Feel Vulnerable When. . ."*

When you leave an abusive partner, you hope that your feeling of vulnerability—your fear of his emotional and physical abuse—will vanish. After all, you're not with him anymore, right? So why should you feel vulnerable? But it's not so easy. You lived with those feelings on a daily basis for a long time, and they're not going to disappear overnight.

One exercise you might try is to view your feelings of vulnerability as something positive rather than negative. As long as you can recognize and learn from these feelings rather than be overwhelmed by them, you have gained a valuable tool to use in your new life.

Think of your feelings as protective warning signals which can alert you to potential danger. For example, after Alicia left Jeff she wanted to sever all connections. However, she was unable to completely avoid contact with Jeff because of his court-ordered child visitation rights. Also, Jeff used the business they still owned together as an excuse to see Alicia. She felt trapped because he was paying child support out of the business revenues and she badly needed the money. Alicia had a persistent feeling of vulnerability which she decided to write about.

I feel vulnerable when I'm in the same room with Jeff. I'm always worried he'll go off the deep end again. I feel especially unsafe when I'm within arm's reach of him, like in the car. When we went to sign the papers for the business, I rode with him in the car. I don't remember what we were talking about, but he "kiddingly" went to punch me in the face. Hah hah, wasn't that funny. Let's pretend to punch Alicia in the face. Hah hah. I just smiled a very tight smile and sort of, well not sort of, I did, zone out. I and my emotions went somewhere for a while. I don't know where. They returned a couple of days later when I remembered the incident. Then the fear I didn't face at the time came back full force. That's when I realized how unsafe the whole situation was, and I made a promise not to put myself in that position again. I hate feeling vulnerable. I want to feel strong and whole and in control of the situation. Or at least in control of myself.

Alicia felt she had to accompany Jeff to sign some papers because they were related to their business, but she recognized that being in the car alone with Jeff put her in a vulnerable situation. Her feelings were borne out when Jeff "kiddingly" punched at her face. For a woman who has been beaten or threatened by a man, a "play" punch is no laughing matter. No matter what the man says, such a gesture is a calculated move on his part to let the woman know he still considers himself in control. In that scary situation, Alicia did what she could to cope: she "zoned out," shutting off her emotions until she felt safe enough to feel them.

When she wrote her piece, Alicia allowed herself to feel the intense fright and vulnerability she had experienced in the car. Her feelings then turned to anger, and she became determined not to put herself in that situation again. She decided that she wanted to feel "strong and whole." When she changed her wish from being "in control of the situation" to "at least in control of myself," she recognized that while she cannot control other people or every situation, she does have control over how she will respond. By examining her feelings of vulnerability, Alicia can more clearly recognize when she is heading into dangerous waters. She can use these insights to make choices that will help her feel "strong and whole." For example, she can choose to have a friend or family member assist when the children are being exchanged for visitation, or have someone besides herself pick them up. If she and Jeff have to go somewhere because of their business, she might decide not to drive with him but to meet him at the destination and perhaps bring along a friend or family member for support.

Your Turn to Write: "I Feel Vulnerable When. . . "

While doing this exercise, create an atmosphere of safety for yourself. This may mean asking a couple of friends to be with you and support you through tough feelings and memories. Maybe sitting in the backyard with your cat sleeping on your lap makes you feel safe, or lying on your bed sipping a warm cup of tea.

Write down your feelings, starting the first line with: "I feel vulnerable when. . . " Remember that whatever you write is valid; none of your feelings or thoughts are trivial or silly. Perhaps you feel vulnerable every time the phone rings, or when you hear the sounds of a ball game coming from the TV because you associate them with your ex-partner. Allow yourself to re-experience what vulnerable feels like. By squarely facing these feelings, you can gain understanding and insight into yourself and your situation.

Think about how to turn your feelings of vulnerability from negative to positive ones. What aspects of your situation that frighten you can you control? What aspects can't you control? What specific choices can you make to keep yourself safe?

4 *Having a Safety Plan*

Imagine that you've been awakened in the middle of the night by the piercing shriek of the smoke detector. You jump out of bed and rush to the children's room. Smoke is billowing up the staircase. Instead of panicking, you and the kids exit through a second-story window that leads you to the back-porch roof, from which you can jump to the ground. You've followed your preplanned emergency escape routine, which you practiced with the kids, and now it has saved your lives.

Many people plan what they would do in case of fire. Hopefully you have, too. But have you planned and rehearsed what you will do if your ex shows up with the intent to harm you or the children? Perhaps you devised a safety plan for yourself and your family when you lived with your abuser: you had a safe place to which you could run if you needed to, a rendezvous point where you would meet your children if you became separated. You memorized emergency phone numbers and kept a spare set of car keys hidden from him. You thought about how you could exit from each room in which he might try to trap you. In short, you were prepared as much as possible.

Now that you're away from him and you're feeling safer, you may not have come up with a safety plan for use in your new home. But, as with preparation in case of fire, isn't it best to be prepared for your ex's unexpected arrival, *just in case?*

Not only is being prepared a good security measure, it also has an added psychological benefit. When you are prepared, you increase your confidence in your ability to handle an emergency. A safety plan can give you a certain amount of peace of mind in that you do not have to always be worrying about what you'll do if he shows up. Go over the safety plan with your children and make sure they understand what to do. If family, friends or neighbors are part of your plan, make sure they understand and agree to what you expect from them.

Your Turn to Write: A Safety Plan

Writing down your safety plan will help make it concrete and consistent. A written plan is clearer for everyone concerned and allows for the opportunity to spot holes or weak points that need to be worked out. Writing out the plan also acknowledges that the threat of your ex's violence is real, not something you're exaggerating.

Try to think of several scenarios you might face. What if

he has a weapon, comes with someone else, crawls in through the bedroom window? What if he has gotten to the switch box and there are no lights, or he's disabled your car? How could you get out? Where would you go? What should the kids do?

Think your plan through, write it out and rehearse it with your children. Go back and revise your written plan if you discover any flaws. Have a trusted friend or family member review it. Decide how often you will review and rehearse your safety plan. Be familiar with it.

5 “My Ex Keeps Doing It: How I Can Protect Myself”

After you’ve left an abusive partner, he may still find ways to harass and abuse you. Despite your best efforts to keep your new address a secret, he may track you down and show up at your door unexpectedly. Sometimes “well-meaning” friends or relatives give him your address or phone number because he’s manipulated them into believing that he really loves you and is sorry about what he did. If you have children together, you probably have to contend with court-ordered visitation. Some abusers use those few moments during visitation exchange to pack in as much verbal abuse as possible.

A typical form of harassment by a former partner is telephone abuse. This can mean obscene calls, hang ups and middle-of-the-night calls. Many women recount the confusion, anxiety and fear they feel when a former partner calls on some pretext and begins putting them down and threatening them. Equally distressing are the calls in which he cries and pleads and tells you how much he loves you and wants you back. There are also those chilling calls in which he threatens to kill himself if you don't return.

It is not unusual to find it very difficult to simply hang up on him during these calls. Perhaps you, as a woman, were brought up not to be rude or to create a scene; perhaps you still rely on your ex-partner's child support; perhaps you're afraid he'll get even more angry if you won't listen to him; perhaps you get caught in old survival patterns of fear and compliance. Many women who have been abused recount hours spent dealing with their ex-partners' telephone abuse and their own seeming inability to hang up. Friends and family may find this response difficult to understand and may become exasperated when you keep "allowing" him to harass you. This in turn may isolate you from the support systems you so need right now.

After being separated from Bill for a year, Anna decided to look at the different ways her ex kept "doing it," including how he manipulated her emotions to make her feel sorry for him or feel hopeful that things would change. She also examined her own contradictory reactions.

Manipulation of emotions
Sorry for him—ha!
Calling collect
Accepting the charges
Hate him
Hopeful
Angry
Maybe, doubts, did it happen?
Nauseated
Listening

Tell him how I feel—let it all out
Thankful for not being with him
Sorry I'm by myself
Angry about the kids
Explaining, still being nice.

Should I hang up?

Thank you for my experiences
Thank you for teaching me not to cry
Thank you for showing me how to hide
Thank you for not being there
Thank you for helping me grow up
Thank you for teaching me unbelievable pain
Thank you for showing me how strong I can be
Thank you so much for not letting me be me
Thank you for hating the words I'm sorry
Thank you for still being there
no matter what.

I wish you would go away
Just leave
I wish I could let go
Show me how to let go
someone, anyone.

I wish I could cry
I wish I knew who I was
I wish I wasn't strong
I wish I could cry
I want to cry.

Thank you for killing the creative me
the naive me
Thank you for teaching me things I

didn't want to know
Thank you for taking me places
I didn't want to go.
All I want is to be left alone
And I'll thank you if you would.

Contradictions like the ones Anna felt are normal, but sometimes they keep you stuck. Anna tried to get herself unstuck by listing all the negatives from her abusive relationship, including things he kept doing. By "thanking" her abuser, she placed the responsibility for his behavior right where it belonged—on him. Giving voice to her fears, frustrations, anger and hope helped Anna take an important step toward letting go of the relationship.

Your Turn to Write: "My Ex Keeps Doing It"

This exercise has two parts. First, write on the topic, "My Ex Keeps Doing It" and see what comes out. Write nonstop for ten minutes; don't pause and don't take your pen away from the paper. Just let it flow. If you get stuck, just write "he keeps doing it" over and over until you can identify what "it" is. "It" could be anything, from giving you a particular look that is loaded with meaning, to threatening to disappear with the kids during visitation, to leaving frightening messages on your answering machine. Being able to see his manipulative behavior for what it really is can be helpful; what is the *purpose* behind his behavior you have chosen to write about? Is he attempting to manipulate your emotions? How do you feel about what he's doing?

Second, write on "How I Can Protect Myself." Make a list of how you have protected yourself from him in the past—did some strategies work better than others? For instance, if he is using telephone abuse to harass you, what about getting an answering machine and screening all your calls? You don't have to be "nice"—you *can* hang up, you *can* call the police.

6 "Someone I Thought I Could Count On Who Disappointed Me"

When you gathered the courage to tell someone about your partner's abuse, who was the first person you confided in? A friend, a sister, a parent, a co-worker? Perhaps it was a hotline counselor or a police officer or your pastor. How did they react?

Hopefully they gave you the support you needed and assured you that the abuse was not your fault. Unfortunately, however, many people are not educated about domestic violence and sometimes the people we confide in disappoint us. Your minister may have urged you to be a better wife. The police officer may have asked what you did to make your partner so mad. Your sister may have shrugged and said, "Well, you *married* the guy." Maybe you and your partner were in couples' counseling and the therapist said you merely had a communication problem. These kinds of responses can be devastating because they reinforce the idea that you are to blame for the abuse.

But you are not to blame for what your ex-partner did to you! The responsibility for his abuse lies solely with him. With that in mind, it's helpful to go back and think about someone you turned to for support who disappointed you. The purpose here is not for you to dredge up and dwell on past hurts, but rather to help you understand your relationships and identify those people who will hinder your journey toward living a violence-free life. Remember that what you are going through now is difficult enough—why make it harder for yourself by being around negative or unsupportive people? (In the next chapter we will look at identifying individuals who will be supportive of your efforts.)

In some cases, you will have to make tough decisions about whether to remain in contact with those who continue to undermine your efforts. You may want to limit contact with them, or limit how much you tell them. In other instances, you may decide to sever the relationships, either temporarily or permanently. When Alicia left Jeff, she turned to her parents for help. Before then, she had kept Jeff's abusive behavior a secret from them. When at last she told them what had been happening, she was flabbergasted and hurt at their reaction.

Dear Mom,

I showed up at your door the day I left Jeff, with a trunkful of clothes and toys and your three grandchildren. I arrived at your house to find you home, and Dad at Jeff's consoling him because I'd left him.

You sat there in your flannel nightgown and asked me why I wouldn't go back. You didn't ask what had happened—you acted as if it didn't matter at all. You were just interested in the fact that

I had left my husband.

So I told you what had happened. You didn't react at all. You very calmly repeated the question, "Why can't you give him a second chance?" That's when I lost it, became hysterical and told you I couldn't, I couldn't, I couldn't, not after what he'd done.

Why couldn't you support me in this decision? Why couldn't you say, just once, "I don't understand, Alicia, but I'm in your corner all the way because I love you and you're my daughter?"

Two years later, after Alicia's divorce was finalized and she was living in another area, her parents continued to invite Jeff to family gatherings. Alicia now says she has given up protesting and instead has worked at setting up a support system of nurturing friends, some of whom she met at a support group for women who had been abused. She rarely discusses her relationship with Jeff with members of her immediate family. She finds that to do so only results in frustration, anger and hurt; her efforts to garner their support have not worked.

Your Turn to Write: "Someone I Thought I Could Count On Who Disappointed Me"

Think about someone you turned to for support who let you down. What made you choose that individual to confide in? How did that person react? How did their response make you feel? How did you deal with the situation?

Do you still have contact with that person? Why or why not?

If you still have a relationship with that person, write

down ideas for how to set boundaries to keep yourself protected from further disappointment. For instance, if you want to maintain a relationship with your brother but he refuses to believe that your ex was abusive to you, you might decide to no longer make any efforts to convince him. Let him know that you would like him to believe you, but for now you accept that he doesn't. State that you will not discuss the subject further with him. Your clearly set boundaries will help protect you from feeling more frustration and pain.

7 "Someone Who Came Through for Me When I Needed Them"

In the previous chapter, you wrote about someone who disappointed you when you turned to them for support. Now you can focus on what happened when you turned to someone for help and they came through for you.

Asking for help can be difficult. Some people believe it shows that they're weak. In reality, though, the opposite is true: asking for help is a sign of strength, because it shows *interdependence*. Interdependence is not the same as dependence, where one individual relies completely on another, but rather a mutual give and take, a situation in which each individual has a certain degree of independence while at the same time relies on the relationship with another. Think about communities that have been hit with a natural disaster, such as a flood. Everyone pitches in to help, rescue, house and feed the flood victims. The community pulls together and rebuilds: this is interdependence.

It can be especially hard to reach out for help if you've been isolated by your partner. It takes tremendous courage to break the silence and reach out to someone, and you should applaud your own efforts. Hopefully you have gotten some supportive responses.

Alicia was devastated by her family's lack of understanding about her leaving Jeff, but she was able to find the support she needed from women she met at a shelter. A year after leaving her husband, Alicia surveyed the steps she had taken and the gains she had made during that period.

I look back on the past year and I see a woman struggling against a mountain built by society. But I've got an army behind me, egging me on. For instance, I've got Louise, who helped me tremendously with my children. When I first got to the shelter, my son wouldn't go to bed until I had changed into my pajamas and had given him my sneakers to take to bed with him. Louise, what do I do? Give him your sneakers, she told me. But he thinks I'm going to leave him. Give him time, Alicia, he needs as much time to get used to the changes as you do. Louise let me know I wasn't a bad mother for leaving, but that I was a good mother for leaving. She has also helped me with the day-to-day problems that arise from being a single mother healing from an abusive marriage.

It was important for Alicia to specifically identify who gave her the support she needed when she left Jeff. This support helped Alicia realize that she was making the right choices for herself and her children and that she was worthy of other people's concern and consideration. The encouragement from her new friends at the shelter helped her through those difficult first months.

Your Turn to Write: "Someone Who Came Through for Me When I Needed Them"

Describe someone who came through for you when you needed them, either while you were still in the abusive relationship or after you left.

What made you decide to reach out to that person? What was it about them that made you decide you could trust them? How did that individual help you? How did their support make a difference in your decision to leave or your commitment not to go back? What would you like to say to that person now?

Note: In the chapter "Finding Support and Making New Friends," we'll talk more about finding people to support you on your journey.

8 "What Might Lure Me Back"

Remember how determined you were, when you first left your partner, never to go back? Perhaps the incident that made you decide to leave was still fresh in your mind—he had taken out his gun and threatened to kill you, or he had called your boss and told her that you were a thief, or he told you he'd take the kids and disappear and you'd never see them again.

But now you've been gone for a while, and you're starting to feel safer. The reason why you left is losing its edge. Maybe you are even beginning to question your decision. *Did I do the right thing? How is he doing without me? Maybe I should give him another chance.*

Leaving a relationship, especially if you have devoted a lot of time, energy and emotion to it, is a complex process. In our society, women are usually the nurturers, the ones who keep intimate relationships thriving. When such a relationship fails, the woman tends to see the failure as her fault, whether this is the case or not. But in a relationship in which there is physical or emotional abuse, the person who is being abusive is wholly responsible for that behavior. You cannot change an abusive person's behavior, only he can do that. If the abusive person refuses to accept responsibility for his behavior, and you decide that you therefore need to end the relationship, you are not "failing" the relationship. Rather, you are taking a very difficult and courageous step toward a healthier life.

When you first leave, you may make statements such as "I'll never go back!" because you feel that way at the time and because you want to be strong. But sometimes you can defeat yourself with such statements because the situation is so complex. For a variety of reasons, you may decide to go back to your partner. Berating yourself about this decision is counterproductive.

Another way of looking at the question of whether or not to return to an abusive partner is to realistically examine what factors might sway you toward returning to your ex. Identifying these factors is the first step toward learning to respond rather than react to them as they surface.

Graciela wrote about her hopes that Hector would miraculously change:

Recently I've been praying that Hector might have a change of heart. How nice it would be not to have to come up against his anger every time he has visitation with Carmen, and I have to be in his presence. A complete change of heart. From none to one. A heart brimming over with support, nurturing, kindness, generosity, helpfulness. Somehow I cannot imagine this man having such a personality transformation. But stranger things have happened. I believe in miracles.

Graciela left and returned to Hector four times before making a final break. Each time she left he would lure her back with "honeymoon" behavior. He bought her gifts, took her out to dinner, showered their daughter, Carmen, with expensive toys and games. Because Graciela so badly wanted to believe that Hector really had changed and had undergone the "personality transformation" she longed for, she was drawn back in. It took her four tries before she finally stopped "believing in miracles" and was able to see his manipulative behavior for what it really was. This doesn't mean that when Hector does something nice for her now that she doesn't feel a twinge of the old hope. But now she is better able to look beyond his actions to his motivations, and usually she doesn't like what she sees.

Your Turn to Write: "What Might Lure Me Back"

If you've left and returned before, you know why you decided to go back. What could convince you to return to your ex-partner this time? Pressure from your family? Lack of money? What if he does something that gives you hope he's changed, such as going to counseling or Alcoholics Anonymous? You may also want to explore your fears—some women feel they might be safer with him, where they can keep an eye on him, rather than away from him where they don't know what he's up to.

As you write about what might make you go back, also explore how realistic it would be for you to do so. Is it really safer to be with him than away from him? Will you really be happier—are the good times good enough to make up for the bad? Are the kids really better off in a home where you're always walking on eggshells and where violence might erupt at any moment? Remember, you and your children do deserve healthy relationships and a peaceful home.

9 Learning to Say No

When you were with your abusive partner, there were probably numerous times when it wasn't safe for you to say no, even when you wanted to. You went along with *his* way of doing things, *his* decisions, whether it was about the clothes you wore or what to eat for dinner, because if you refused you ran the risk of listening to him rant and rave about how horrible you were, or being locked out of the house or car, or being hit. By refraining from saying no in the abusive relationship, you were protecting yourself. For Graciela, the most significant times around this issue were when Hector wanted to have sex.

Hector would tell me there was something wrong with me if I didn't want to make love (have sex) a couple of times a day, or if I didn't want to do it his way, even if it was painful for me. If I said no, there'd be hell to pay, worse than the pain I felt from giving in.

Now that you're away from your ex-partner, it's important to start learning how to say no when appropriate. Learning to assert yourself this way is not easy, especially since it was unsafe to do while with your ex-partner. Also, women are socialized to please others, to keep things running smoothly by not rocking the boat. When a co-worker asks you for the umpteenth time to stay late to help her with work she's behind on, you may feel you can't decline because you don't want her to get mad at you. Maybe you're the parent who's always making ten dozen chocolate chip cookies for your child's team bake sale. Perhaps you're the member of the car pool who always takes more turns driving than anybody else. If you find it hard to say no in these situations, remember that someone else did, otherwise *you* wouldn't be doing all the work. Breaking the pattern of just going along with what others want will make you less vulnerable to being taken advantage of, either by your ex or by someone else.

Your Turn to Write: Learning to Say No

This exercise has three parts. First, write about times in your relationship when it was dangerous for you to say no. What kinds of behaviors or activities did you go along with that you didn't want to? Drinking or taking drugs with your ex? Punishing the kids more severely than you thought was right? Dressing a certain way because it was how he wanted you to look? How did you feel when you went along with his agenda, even though you didn't want to and it hurt or humiliated you? What would have happened if you had said no to his demands?

Next, write about an incident in your life, not related to your ex and which has happened since you left him, when you said yes and you really wanted to say no—and when it would have been safe to do so. For instance, after you agreed to let your sister do her laundry at your house because her washing machine was broken, did *you* get stuck doing it because she left to have her hair cut? Did your neighbor ask you to pick up a few items when you went to the grocery store, and then present you with a two-page list after you'd said yes? What would have happened if you had said no in these scenarios? Compare these instances with what would have happened if you had said no to your abuser. How are these situations different?

Finally, imagine a future scenario in which you are asked to say yes but instead you say no! Choose a situation in which it is safe for you to say no. When saying no, don't get caught up in lengthy explanations about why you aren't agreeing. Just say, "No, I can't" or "I'm sorry, but the answer is no"; if you feel you must, give a brief reason, such as "I'll have to say no, I already have dinner plans." If the person persists, simply repeat what you've already said.

Take a deep breath and write your scenario; put it into dialogue form, like a play:

Scenario

A friend calls me one afternoon. She has three children and frequently asks me to baby-sit, without ever offering to pay me or baby-sit my daughter in exchange. I'm really beginning to feel that she takes advantage of me. I've never said no to her before.

Friend: I know this is the night you go to your exercise class, but I was wondering if you'd skip it; I really need you to baby-sit for me.

Me: No, sorry, I can't.

Friend: Couldn't you skip it just this once? Aaron just called and asked me to the movies.

Me: I'm sorry, but I've made a commitment to myself not to miss any of these classes. I'm going to have to say no.

Friend: Come on, couldn't you do it just this once?

Me: No, I can't, I already have a commitment.

Friend: Please, just this once?

Me: No, I can't.

How did it feel to say no in your scenario? How was saying no here different from when you wanted to say no to your ex when you were still with him? You can strengthen your skill at saying no by coming up with more scenarios like this and practicing them with a friend with whom you feel comfortable.

PART II

What Happened:
Remembering, Grieving, Letting Go

10 "Why I Left"

When a woman leaves her abusive partner and is on her own, she often finds herself questioning whether she did the right thing. She may have internalized the societal messages that dictate that a mother should strive to keep her family together or that a woman needs to have a man. Even if she doesn't agree with these beliefs, it can be hard at first to be alone.

You may be wondering if you should answer the letter your ex-partner recently sent you describing how much he misses you and stating that things will be different if only you would come back. Perhaps your children keep saying how much they miss Daddy and your heart breaks all over again when you remember the good times you experienced together as a family. Or perhaps he's still harassing you, and you begin to think, "What's the point? I may be on my own, but he's still harassing me and to top it all off, *he's* got the house and the car."

Many people do not realize how difficult it is for a woman who has lived with an abusive partner to leave and start a new life on her own. It takes a strong, courageous woman to do this.

You are this woman! You have worked hard to keep yourself and your children safe. You made the difficult decision to leave. And now here you are, on your own. Beginning a new life is full of everyday challenges and a whirlwind of emotions. There is nothing wrong with feeling both excited and worried about being on your own, feeling relief that your ex is gone and at the same time missing him and the decent parts of your life together. It's all right to feel conflicted. These contradictory feelings are normal, but it's important for you to be aware of them, because they may make you vulnerable to going back to your ex-partner.

Now is the time to sit down and think about why you decided to leave him in the first place. Writing on the topic "Why I Left" will help you remember and explore what was unhealthy about your relationship with your abusive partner, and why you needed to get away.

Maggie still loves her ex-boyfriend, Russell, and every day she struggles with her feelings. Sometimes it's difficult for her to focus on why she decided to break away from him. Writing down her specific reasons for leaving has helped her recognize just how bad the situation had gotten with Russell, and has given her the resolve not to see him ever again.

I left Russell because of his abusive behaviors. I couldn't deal with his severe discipline of the kids and his constant ridicule and put-downs about me as a parent, partner and housekeeper—demeaning, painful words that purposefully hurt me. My children

and I were living in fear of his anger and violence. He controlled everything and everyone in the house, and outsiders (family and friends) were made to feel awkward every time they called or visited. I saw my life being taken from me with his control and power tactics. The love that was shared was a string he'd pull and take with no giving in return at the end. So, out of fear for our lives (the kids'and mine) and love for my children, I left.

Your Turn to Write: "Why I Left"

Think about why you left your partner. In what kinds of ways was he behaving? How was he treating you? How did his behavior make you feel, both emotionally and physically? Don't censor anything. Let yourself feel what you were feeling then (hurt, sorrow, rage, confusion) and describe those emotions. Let yourself cry if you need to. You may want to set up some support in advance—for example, arrange to talk to a friend after you've completed this writing.

11 The Last Straw

It may have been two in the morning and he came home drunk and took out his deer rifle and started screaming that he knew you were sleeping around and he was going to blow your head off. . .

It may have been a freezing night and he threw you outside in your nightgown and bare feet because he didn't like your asking for money to buy your son's birthday present. . .

It may have been at a back-yard barbecue at a friend's house where he slapped you and called you a fat slob in front of everybody because he decided he didn't like the shorts you were wearing. . .

It may have been. . .

The specific incident that made you take action on your plans for leaving your abuser may not have been the most violent, the most humiliating or the most dangerous thing he ever did. Or it may have been all of those things. Either way, it felt like a culmination of the abuse he had dished out over the course of your relationship: the last straw. It gave you the motivation to finally get free.

You now know that time and absence can dilute not only your fear, but also your memories. In your new life away from your abuser, you forget how bad it was; you may even start to miss him. As noted in the previous chapter, this can be a time when you are vulnerable to the possibility of returning to your partner, even if you know in your head that you should not return. One way to keep the relationship in perspective is to remember the specific reason that made you say, "Enough! I'm leaving."

Graciela left Hector several times before she got free of him for good. She wanted to understand this pattern so that she could make healthier choices in her new life. Also, there were times when she still felt a pull in her heart toward Hector, especially in the late evening after Carmen was asleep and the company of the television or a book just wasn't enough.

I remember one night Hector had been in my face for hours, wearing me down mentally. He had made me take the groceries back to the store because I had gotten more items than were on his list. When I got home he started in on me for something else. This went on well into the night. He started backing me into corners and saying I was crazy and that he was going to take Carmen away from me. I was probably hysterical by then. I called the police. They came and took one look at me—I probably did look like a lunatic after all those hours of mental abuse—and they looked at Hector—cool as a cucumber, not a hair ruffled—and they told me I should leave. They gave me no support

whatsoever. I felt completely abandoned. They said I had no reason to press charges because they saw nothing wrong with me. Then they shook hands with Hector and left.

I left when they did and went to the shelter. It was my fifth trip there and it was the last one.

The events Graciela describes had probably happened many times before, but something about this particular time was different. Maybe it was the police officers' attitude. Perhaps Graciela had just had enough, enough hours of Hector's screaming at her, enough of his controlling her by raging at things like her buying something at the grocery store that was not on his list. Perhaps she had had enough of being viewed by the police as a "hysterical" woman while he was able to appear unruffled. Whatever the exact impetus, it propelled her out of the abusive relationship and into freedom.

Your Turn to Write: The Last Straw

This is a difficult exercise. It asks you to relive the emotion-laden event that made you decide to leave. While you're writing, remember that you already took action and that you're safe now. Keep in mind your strength and your courage—you must have both to have survived what he did to you. Check that your support system will be available for you when you're done writing.

Now, take a deep breath and write about the incident that made you decide you had to leave. (You may not have left immediately after it, as Graciela did, but it was a turning point in your process of getting free.) Use detail. Where were you? Describe the place. What was the time of day or night? What time of year? What were you doing when this happened? What was the expression on your abuser's face? How did you feel, physically and emotionally?

What was the next step you took?

While you're writing, keep breathing.

12 *"Why I Stayed"*

Perhaps the most commonly asked question about women in abusive relationships is "Why do they stay?" Doesn't this question really annoy you? Like anyone in a relationship, you had feelings for your partner. In the beginning, he probably didn't come across as abusive and may have been devoted and romantic. The ongoing relationship wasn't *always* bad.

Maybe you had children and wanted to keep the family together, or you and the children needed the added financial support. Sometimes people outside the relationship have a hard time recognizing these factors as reasons for staying, and they ask, "Why didn't you just leave?" even when they should know better. You may just have to accept that these people do not understand your situation, and move on rather than get frustrated with them.

When you're trying to sort out your feelings after you've

left an abusive relationship, you may buy into the assumption that leaving is easy and start to criticize yourself for having stayed as long as you did. Time and distance can make the reasons you stayed seem less compelling. You begin to forget how afraid you were or how strong your attachment to him was. The question "Why *did* I stay?" haunts you.

It is as important to remember why you stayed as it is to recall why you left. Remembering why you stayed helps to put all the parts of your relationship into proper perspective. Maggie had just left Russell when she wrote the following piece about why she'd spent half a year with him. You may recognize your own story in Maggie's description of how Russell was wonderful at first but gradually proved to be critical and controlling.

In the beginning everything seemed like a dream come true. Love, kindness, willingness, communication, all the things that made me feel wonderful and special. He gave me gifts, flowers, dinners, dates and compliments. Along with all that he let me know how concerned he was about me, asking questions such as "How are you doing? Is there anything I can do?" And he took some of the responsibilities that can be overbearing. Then, when I felt this person was great and wonderful and helpful, he started questioning me, as if he was concerned. I said to myself, "Ah, this is so nice," but then I realized it was not so nice.

He started making up excuses, or saying how sorry he was or that he would change. This kept me hoping. Then came the blows to my self-esteem, my judgments and parenting decisions.

. . .

Your Turn to Write: "Why I Stayed"

You've already written about why you left. Now, write about why you stayed. Try not to be judgmental with yourself. Instead, try to be open and honest as you explore the reasons that kept you with your ex.

Using what you have learned about what kept you in the relationship with an abusive partner, how might you deal with those factors if a similar situation in a relationship happened now? How might you use your experience with your ex-partner to make decisions about the new relationship?

13 "I'm Not Crazy—There Were Good Times, Too"

For many women who have left abusive partners, friends and family members who had been urging you to leave are now heaving huge sighs of relief. "Whew, that's over, she's OK now and I can get back to my own life." You are grateful for their support, but sometimes isn't it just a little too much? Isn't their applause just a little too loud? You get nervous about potential failure. You're afraid they'll be disappointed in you if you decide to go back, and that you'll feel ashamed.

And maybe they just can't seem to understand why, at times, you miss your ex and think about him in a wistful, loving manner. They act as if there's something wrong with you for feeling this way. "What, are you crazy? After all that horrible stuff he did to you? Forget about him. You're better off without him."

While it probably is true that you're better off without

him, it's upsetting when no one seems to understand your complicated feelings for your ex-partner. After all, you already know you needed to end the relationship; otherwise you wouldn't have decided to leave in the first place. But what do you do with those tender, nostalgic feelings you still have for your ex?

First, recognize that it's perfectly normal and OK for you to feel these pangs. You probably invested a lot of emotional energy in the relationship and tried hard to make it work. It is unrealistic to think you can just let go of those feelings overnight. A lot of women worry about having these feelings and begin to think something is wrong with them. "How can I still care about him after what he's done to me? I must really be messed up. Maybe I really did like being abused."

You're not messed up and you didn't enjoy the abuse! Most likely you're holding onto the good parts of the relationship, not the bad. To see this more clearly, try to separate out in your mind the good times from the bad. For example, perhaps in the beginning of your relationship your partner was loving and attentive and did everything he could to please you. It's that person whom you miss, not the one who slapped you across the face because he couldn't find the remote control.

Alicia came up with the following:

I remember one day we were in the house and a song came on the radio. I don't remember which one, now. We held each other close and slow-danced in the middle of the living room with the children playing and toys all over the floor. It was the most tender moment of our marriage, just holding each other close and slowly swaying to the music.

Remembering the good times means honoring what was positive about the relationship and your efforts to sustain it. Remembering the good times lets you know that you were *not* crazy, that there were worthwhile aspects of the relationship which made you stay in it. The catch here is that while it's helpful to remember the good times, you must put these memories into perspective and realize that, ultimately, all of the good times in your relationship can not make up for the abuse.

Remember the good times, grieve over them and for the healthy relationship you longed for but were denied—and prepare to move on.

Your Turn to Write: "I'm Not Crazy—There Were Good Times, Too"

What were the good times that kept you in your relationship? Describe one significant moment as Alicia did, or make a whole list of memories. Allow yourself to feel the giddy happiness you felt when you and your partner first fell in love. Allow yourself to feel the warmth of shared intimacies—special moments that seemed to make up for everything else.

Also allow yourself to feel grief, betrayal and anger over the loss of those good times and the healthy relationship you had hoped for and which your partner made impossible by his decision to be abusive. Remember, you are mourning the death of your relationship and it's OK to cry.

14 "*What My Life Would Be Like If I Hadn't Left*"

We've already looked at many of the factors that might make you go back to your ex-partner and the factors that keep you away. Perhaps right now your resolve never to return is very strong. But you may also retain a glimmer of hope that you will get back together with him and that your relationship will somehow work out.

It takes a lot for an abusive man to change. Giving up power and control, especially when our society lets those who have it get away with so much, is not easy. Has he been regularly attending a group for violent men? You may want to contact your area's domestic violence program and find out if they think the local batterers' program is a good one. Even if he is attending a group, it is a long, difficult process to change abusive behaviors. Motivation is the key here. *You* really want to change. Does he?

Whenever you feel the glimmer of hope that your relationship will be different, it may be helpful to think about what your life would be like if you had never left. Some women believe they would not be alive at all. Considering that every day four women are killed in the U.S. by intimate partners, these women are being neither paranoid nor overly dramatic. Graciela is one of the women who believes she would have ended up dead—either physically or in spirit—if she remained with her abuser.

Judging by the way things were going the day I left Hector for good, I probably would be in the river now and that would be a step up. Medicated and zombied out due to snapping mentally and physically, I probably would be smoking a pack or two of cigarettes a day. To numb the pain and horror I probably would have picked up a drink. I pray not. The guilt, self-doubt and insanity I would feel probably would have a tremendous effect on my daughter and most likely she would not be the same child she is today. I would feel unloved and unable to love. All hope would have receded far into the past, and me with it.

I would become one of the walking wounded or walking dead.

Your Turn to Write: "What My Life Would Be Like If I Hadn't Left"

This is one of the exercises in which it's important for you to first make yourself feel as safe and comfortable as possible. Remember that you are OK now and that you chose to leave, not stay. Write about what your life would be like right now if you had stayed with your abusive partner. Allow yourself to feel whatever you believe you would be feeling—despair, hopelessness, fear, love, anger, continued hope. What would your health be like? Your relationships with your children, friends and family? What would your future have held?

In your mind's eye, let the person who is the "you-who-never-left" look into your bathroom mirror. Who is it that you see?

15 *A Letter to Your Abuser*

There were many remarks you never made to your abuser because you were afraid of the consequences. You kept your innermost feelings to yourself. Sometimes you buried those feelings so effectively that even you did not know what they really were.

How many times since you've left have you wanted to call him and tell him how much you hate him, how much you love him, how much you miss him, how you wish he'd disappear off the face of the earth? Perhaps you want him to acknowledge how much pain, fear and aggravation he has caused you. Maybe you want him to understand how his behavior has affected the kids. It is possible that you want him to comprehend just how much he lost when his behavior caused you to leave.

It still may not be safe for you to say any of this directly to him; you will have to decide for yourself whether it's worth taking the chance. Not only would you risk his negative reaction, you would also risk becoming involved with him again. Whenever you have an emotion-filled interaction with your ex-partner, whether positive or negative, it can activate the old patterns and reassert the bond between you.

A safer alternative is to write a letter to your ex which you never send to him. By deciding this beforehand, you automatically create a safe space for yourself to express your feelings about the relationship and your ex's abusive behavior. Because he will never see it, you don't have to "pretty it up" in order to protect yourself or spare his feelings. You can speak from the heart and from the gut.

After she left, Anna wrote Bill such a letter, which she never mailed, as a way to get the weight of her feelings off her chest. In her letter, you can hear Anna's frustration over Bill's lack of good parenting of their children and over his continuing to blame her for "everything that went wrong or is going wrong in your life." She concluded by pointing out that Bill is responsible for his own life.

Bill:

Where do you get off hassling me about not being able to talk to your kids? I can't afford to accept your collect calls and legally I don't have to. What's wrong with your hand? You can't write them a letter? Josh and Ashley are still upset that you forgot their birthday. And neither of them will forget about Christmas. Why are you so worried about talking to your kids now? You weren't worried about them then.

I've been taking care of our kids for a year by myself. And yes, it was my choice. And you know what? The kids and I are a whole lot happier now than we ever were. Every time I hear your voice, it makes me want to puke. And I don't care what you think, I had nothing to do with your ending up in jail. And you know what? I

don't really care. Stop blaming me for everything that went wrong or is going wrong in your life. You made your own choices. Now you can live with them.

—Anna

Your Turn to Write: A Letter to Your Abuser

First, in order to give yourself the freedom and safety to really express what's in your heart and mind, make a decision that you will not give your abuser this particular letter, no matter how tempting it might be.

Now, start writing. Once you've started, try to write continuously, without stopping. Picture your words as water rushing from a broken dam: plentiful, forceful, unstoppable.

Your letter may be angry, contemplative, sad, hurt or any combination of feelings. Your relationship with your ex-partner was complex and your letter may reflect your conflicting behaviors and emotions. On the other hand, your letter may be short, one or two lines which sum up your dominant emotions or the message you want to convey to your ex. Don't be afraid to express contradictory feelings such as, "I miss you but I never want to see you again."

16 A Letter to Someone Significant in Your Life About What Happened

Some women decide to keep the abuse in their relationships a secret. But many tell family and friends. Chances are there are people close to you who were affected by your being abused.

Think about how it pains your heart when someone you love has been hurt in some way. Because you care about them, you empathize with their distress. If your child comes in crying after being taunted by the neighborhood bully, if your brother calls to tell you he's just been laid off from his job, if your girlfriend's mother dies, you empathize with them and share their pain. This is a healthy way of loving and caring about others.

There are people in your life who care about you and who empathize with your pain. They may be your mom and dad, who stood by you and let you know their door was always open; your girlfriend who let you sleep on her couch and who listened to your grief late into the night; your minister who helped you understand that if you were being hurt and humiliated, then your husband had broken the sacred covenant of your marriage; or your children who bravely left their home to chart unfamiliar territory with you so that you could be safe. These people care about you and that is a precious gift.

What would you like to say to these people? Maybe you'd like to tell them how much their support has meant to you. Or there may be someone who doesn't really understand what you went through, or what you're going through now, and you'd like to tell that person in your own words what it's been like for you.

Maggie wanted to tell her children just how much they meant to her; she also wanted to provide them with an explanation about what had happened and why she had made certain choices that affected them.

Dear Meagan and Robert:

I love you with all my heart. You are the most precious part of my life. I feel you should know this.

I am writing you this letter to explain why I decided it was time to help make your lives and mine healthier, one step at a time.

The reason I decided to come to the women's shelter was to protect you from the abuse you've encountered from Russell and change things the best I can. I want you to know that abuse of any kind is not OK for a woman or child to have to live with. You are the most important person to yourselves and no one has the right to do anything to you that is hurtful. Life is the most precious gift that God has given you and you're not supposed to be harmed by anyone. I hope all the love and support we get now will help all of us be happy and healthy.

Love you always, Mom

Your Turn to Write: A Letter to Someone Significant in Your Life About What Happened

Write a letter to someone significant in your life (not your ex) about what happened to you when you were with your abusive partner or when you left him.

What about your experience do you want the person you're addressing to understand? Think about what made you pick this person to write to, and make that part of your letter, too. How does this person fit into your support system?

You can decide if you want to share your letter with the person you've written to. Remember, don't share your letter if it will jeopardize your physical or emotional safety.

17 Letting Go

If someone you loved died, people would be sympathetic and supportive of your grief. Similarly, if you lost your home and all your possessions—including treasures such as photographs and family keepsakes—in a fire, most people would be very sympathetic to your loss. Mourning over losses such as these is socially acceptable, and no one thinks your grief is strange.

Women who have been abused often have endured multiple losses: bonds with friends and family members broken; jobs, homes, possessions and pets left behind; children taken away; sobriety, self-esteem, peace of mind eroded. But mourning these kinds of losses is not socially acceptable; you may have experienced a negative reaction if you expressed your grief over the ending of your relationship with your ex-partner.

But you are dealing with the loss of a significant relationship and need to take the time to grieve over this loss so that you can let it go and move on.

Your Turn to Write: Letting Go

For this exercise, you will write a eulogy for your relationship. A eulogy traditionally contains words of tribute and remembrance honoring someone who has died. You can also compose a eulogy for any thing or person you have lost, such as your relationship with your ex-partner. Writing a eulogy gives you the opportunity to reflect on your life with your ex-partner, and to express your feelings about losing that person. It is a way to put formal closure on your relationship with your ex-partner.

Here are some suggestions for beginning your eulogy:

"I have come to the point where I need to say good-bye once and for all and to let you go."

"I never thought I'd say this, but I am letting you go, completely and utterly."

As you write, think of your words as bricks in a wall that you are building between your old relationship and your new life. One by one they connect to form a strong, protective barrier. You are on this side of the barrier; you are safe.

When you finish your eulogy, consider having a ceremony to honor what it stands for. Gather together some friends and read the eulogy to them. Maybe you'd like to share it with members of your support group for women who have been abused, or with a significant person who supported you in getting free of your ex-partner. It may be a private ceremony with just you present. Alicia, for instance, took her wedding ring to the woods, buried it under a tree and read her eulogy to Jeff over it. Do something that has personal significance for you, that you find comforting and healing.

18 "What I Like Best About My New Life"

In Part II, you have spent a lot of time and emotional energy looking at your relationship with your ex-partner for what it really was. To wrap up, take a deep breath and shift back to the here and now; focus for a moment on what you enjoy most about your new life.

Alicia said that one of the most delightful aspects of her new life was being able to put the furniture wherever she wanted. When she lived with Jeff, he had dictated where everything had to be, and if anything was moved he would "punish" Alicia. During the first few weeks in her new apartment, Alicia rearranged the furniture every day, just for the pleasure of being able to do so without fear.

Anna said what she liked best about her new life was not having to worry about where the television remote control was. When she was with Bill, he hit her if he couldn't find it.

What Alicia and Anna identify as the best parts of their new lives may seem small on the surface, but they represent something much, much larger: safety and freedom.

Your Turn to Write: "What I Like Best About My New Life"

Make a list of all the aspects of your new life that you are enjoying, such as:

"I can go to bed when I want to, not when he says I can."

"I don't have to keep the children quiet all the time the way I had to around my ex."

"I don't have to be constantly nervous and anxious anymore."

"I can have friends over—he never let me."

"I have control over my own life again."

Put your list where you will see it every day—by your bed, in your car or on your closet door, for instance. Whenever you feel down or overwhelmed or ready to give up and go back to your ex-partner, read through your list. Take the time to reflect not only on what you've written, but also on what it represents: freedom, safety and a healthier life for yourself and your children.

PART III

Moving On: Finding Out What You Really Want for Yourself

Section I

Healthy Relationships

19 The Difference Between Being Lonely and Being Alone

Being by yourself isn't all that bad. Before last year, I always had to have a man hanging around or I felt unloved. Having someone in my life and having him stuck to me like glue gave me a false sense of security, and created tremendous fear, loneliness and isolation. This time, though, I'm enjoying my solitude, getting to know myself, gardening, cooking for myself. I never thought I'd be able to survive very long without a man around. But guess what? I'm doing just fine!

—Graciela

Throughout history, women have had little freedom to make their own way in the world; most went from their father's home into that of their husband. Women were dependent upon men for support and protection.

Today, in this country, women have achieved much greater independence. Vast numbers of women are employed in the workforce and many women are the sole breadwinners for their families. Even so, outdated ideas, such as a woman needs to be protected by a man or that she isn't a "total" woman without one, persist in our society.

Certainly many of us yearn for the love, companionship and connectedness of a healthy relationship with a man. Probably that's what you were looking for when you became involved with your ex-partner. Sometimes, however, you can enter a relationship for the wrong reasons. One of these reasons is often the fear of being alone and being lonely.

But *aloneness* and *loneliness* are two very different states of being. Think about your former relationship. Weren't there many times when you were lonely, even with him sitting right there or sleeping next to you at night? Being with someone does not necessarily mean an end to loneliness and being alone does not have to mean being lonely.

Being alone can mean having the opportunity to explore who *you* are and what *you* want and need because you aren't always having to answer your partner's demands. Having uninterrupted time to yourself provides you with the opportunity to nurture yourself; for example, to read a book, take a soothing bath, meditate or walk. Being alone gives you the space to dream.

Alicia lived with her parents until she married Jeff at age eighteen. When Jeff's abuse made Alicia realize that she had to leave, she found herself facing her fear of loneliness. After taking the first steps toward setting up an independent life for herself and her children, Alicia began to realize that being without a romantic companion did not mean that she had to be lonely.

There is fear in loneliness. There is the fear of looking inside

yourself and seeing a void, a desert of sand and monotonous boredom. The fear that accompanies the emptiness you feel, and trying to dispel that emptiness, sometimes frantically. You grasp at anything and anyone to fill up the emptiness: TV droning as you hypnotically stare at the tube; calling friends and acquaintances to talk and chatter away the time. You get off the phone and you can't remember a damn thing of importance you or they had said. Inviting a man over to spend the night and you really can't stand the bastard, all he talks about is himself, his work, his life as you absent-mindedly nod your head occasionally so that he thinks you're listening.

Use the time to rediscover yourself. Take a walk and see what you can find. Read books about things you are interested in. Don't escape into trash novels, it won't dispel the loneliness, only make it worse when you come to the end of the book. Dump dead-end friends and find people you can laugh with. Write a book about how you feel or draw a picture.

Being alone can strengthen rather than drain you. Being alone can feel wonderful.

Your Turn to Write: The Difference Between Being Alone and Being Lonely

Write about what you see as the difference between being alone and being lonely. You might think of the messages you've received from society, family or your abuser that have influenced how you think about being alone.

What are the good aspects of being alone? Maybe, like Alicia, you will use your time alone as an opportunity to rediscover yourself. How might you go about this? Maybe you will use some of Alicia's suggestions.

Even in a healthy relationship, individuals need time alone for rest, reflection and rejuvenation. Remember to take that time for yourself. It's not selfish, but rather a positive way to enrich your life and your relationships with others.

20 Caring or Controlling?

"He's so romantic—he calls me every hour just to say hi, sometimes even until two in the morning!"

"He wants us to spend all our free time together. He's even jealous of any time I spend with my girlfriends. I think he *really* loves me."

"He got so furious when he saw an old picture of me and my ex-boyfriend that he made me set fire to it in the sink. After, we made love and it was great. That night he told me there'll never be anybody else for him but me. He's so intense it's a little scary, but nobody's ever cared as much about me as he does."

Why do we sometimes confuse behavior that is controlling for behavior that is caring? Controlling behavior often masquerades as romantic or caring. Many popular books and movies promote this image—remember the scene in the classic film *Gone With the Wind*, where Rhett subdues

Scarlett and then carries her up the stairs to have his way with her? The next morning, the strong-willed, intelligent Scarlett has been transformed into a simpering wife, presumably because of a night of forced sex. "Ah," the audience sighs, "How romantic!"

It's natural to want the man you care for to pay attention to you. If your life isn't going so well, you may crave that attention even more. If you look back at your relationship, especially the beginning, you will probably see behaviors which you now understand to be controlling but which at the time seemed to be indicators of how much he cared for you.

Maggie reviewed her first weeks with Russell, which, while being lived, had seemed really wonderful. She remembered how he always insisted on driving whenever they went anywhere, even though it was Maggie's car. He told Maggie she worked too hard and that the least he could do was to drive and let her relax. He started driving her to and from work; when she went grocery shopping, he drove and waited in the car until she was finished. Maggie realized that Russell was using apparent caring behavior to control her by keeping tabs on her every movement.

Your Turn to Write: Caring or Controlling?

Look back at your relationship with your ex-partner, especially its beginning. Can you see behaviors of your ex-partner which at the time seemed to indicate how much he cared about you but were really mechanisms of control? Make a list of these behaviors. What has made you realize the difference between *care* and *control*? Don't get down on yourself for having been taken in; it is often very difficult to sort out what are controlling and possessive behaviors while in the midst of a relationship, especially in those first heady weeks when everything seems so good and hopeful. Before putting your list away, add at least five more examples of a man's controlling behavior that at first seems romantic: he frequently drops by your house or office unannounced, he always wants to pick out the clothes you wear, he insists you snuggle next to him in the car even though it means you're uncomfortable and you can't wear your safety belt.

When or if you start dating again, review your list of controlling behaviors. Use the knowledge you've gained from your experiences and look at new relationships with a clear perspective. Work at keeping a balance between healthy skepticism and openness to potentially healthy relationships. The chapter entitled "What I Want in a Relationship" at the end of this section will help you sort out what you want and don't want in a new relationship.

21 The Difference Between Being Taken Care Of and Being Supported

It feels so good, sometimes, to let someone else take care of our lives for us. Can't stand dealing with the bills? How nice to have him tell you not to worry yourself about it, that he'll handle all the finances—just sign your paycheck over to him every week. Find it a hassle to shop for the best car insurance and keep up with the premiums? What a relief when he says he'll take care of this—if you'll just sign the title over to him, he'll be more than happy to put your car on his policy.

But is this really so nice? Sure, it's lovely to feel that someone cares enough about you to help shoulder some of the responsibilities, but when does this kind of "help" cross the line from a healthy sharing of responsibilities to an unhealthy dynamic of power and control?

Sometimes we mistake being taken care of for being supported. It's not easy to see the difference, because these two behaviors look very similar. But in reality, they are significantly different.

When you're being taken care of, *you give up control*. When you're being supported, *you retain control*. In this regard, *control* means the freedom to make your own decisions, big and small, about how to live your life. In an unhealthy relationship one partner may try to make the other dependent upon them in order to maintain control. In a healthy and balanced interdependent relationship, the two partners are mutually supportive of each other.

For instance, let's say you want to take an evening class in managing personal finances. In an unhealthy relationship your partner might say he's supportive of your going, but points out that the classes are expensive, and, besides, he'd be worried about you driving there at night. He has a better idea: since he knows all about financial investing, why doesn't he handle your money for you? That way you won't have to go to the class and you can have more time together! In a healthy, supportive relationship, on the other hand, your partner might congratulate you on wanting to learn more about managing your money, agree to prepare dinner and put the kids to bed on the evening of your class and follow through on his promise each week. Maybe you agree to do the same on a different night so that he can have time to himself to go to the gym or take a class also.

Graciela eventually learned to make this important distinction:

Being taken care of to me means someone else taking care of my responsibilities. Being taken care of means turning control of my life over to someone else, willingly or not, and having that person run my life. To me, being supported means

someone supporting my decision-making about the direction, focus and action that I want for my life.

Your Turn to Write: The Difference Between Being Taken Care Of and Being Supported

What, for you, is the difference between being taken care of and being supported? Think about relationships you've had throughout your life, not just the romantic ones. Which ones fit into which category and why? How did these relationships affect you? Did they make you feel able to meet the challenges of life, or did they make you feel you needed somebody to do it for you? What do you want from future relationships?

22 Sex and Intimacy

You can be as physically close as making love or on opposite sides of a room at a dinner party, and still feel the other person holding you. Holding your heart in their hand, and you feel safe and warm with quiet joy.

—Alicia

What is it that you hope for when you become sexually active with someone? Certainly there's the physical pleasure that sex can bring. Often, for women, becoming sexual with someone they're dating is synonymous with becoming more intimate. A new bond is formed, a new level of connectedness is reached. Sometimes, though, women get involved sexually with a man because they are looking to fill another need, such as loneliness or low self-esteem.

Now that you're on your own, you may find yourself especially vulnerable to starting a sexual relationship before you feel truly ready for it, or with someone who's not appropriate for you. Perhaps you feel lonely, or you're still afraid of your ex and believe that you'd be safer if another man was around. Maybe you're wondering if another man will find you attractive.

Before getting involved sexually, think about what it is you really need in your life now. If you're currently sexually involved, take a step back and think about what you want—and what you are getting—from the relationship.

Your Turn to Write: Sex and Intimacy

How have your own views on sex and intimacy influenced your choice of when, with whom and how you get sexually involved? What do you think you are looking for when you become sexually involved? Physical pleasure? Companionship? A deepening of intimacy with a significant other? Validation or approval? A shared experience that will give your relationship an added richness? Make your own list.

Did you find what you were looking for in your previous relationships? What can you do to help make the best decision for yourself about when to become sexually involved, and whether you are getting what you need and want, once you are involved?

A woman can and should celebrate her sexuality in ways that give her pleasure, while also maintaining her safety and protecting her health. Sexually transmitted diseases are widespread and can have consequences ranging from infertility to death; the AIDS epidemic is spreading fastest among women. Educate yourself on these health issues and *use what you learn*. A condom left in your purse because he says he doesn't like them isn't going to do you any good.

Many women who have been abused had the right to say no to unsafe sex taken away from them by their violent partners. If this was your situation, do not blame yourself or feel you should have somehow taken better care of yourself. It was not your fault. Try to focus on taking the best possible care of yourself *now*.

23 *"What I Want in a Relationship"*

"I'm through with men!" "No more relationships!" "Never again!" How many women have uttered these words after a breakup? These statements sum up all the feelings of disappointment, betrayal, rage and hurt, while at the same time express determination never to let it happen again. For women who have been abused, these declarations also voice the desire to feel safe and respected.

If you decide to get involved with a man after leaving an abusive partner, it's good to clearly identify what you do want in a relationship as well as what you don't want. It's easy to repeat or get stuck in old patterns, unless you pay attention to the warning signs of a potentially abusive relationship. Warning signs are behaviors that indicate that the person may be abusive or controlling. Does this man ask your opinion about what movie you'd like to see or what restaurant you'd like to eat in or does he decide for the two of you? Does he constantly interrupt you when you're talking or dismiss your opinions as silly or trivial? Does he make jokes or derogatory comments about women? Does he speak about his mother disrespectfully? Has he had trouble holding a job and blames it on everyone but himself? Does he blame all the breakups of his previous relationships on the women? Does he mistreat animals? Pay attention to these kinds of indicators *before* you get too deeply involved with him.

Another way to approach a potential new relationship is to set some criteria for the man you might get involved with and think about what kind of relationship you want. When Alicia started thinking about dating again after the breakup of her marriage, she found it helpful to write out what she didn't want in a new relationship as well as what she did. She used two of her previous relationships, her marriage and her relationship with an abusive boyfriend, to identify what she wanted to avoid.

I don't want one like the last one. No manipulation, deceit, constant yelling. I don't want one like my marriage. Fists, hands closing around my throat and my mind, sneers, yells, boozy breath, objects being thrown and broken, including myself. I don't hold out much hope for a good relationship, but I want a man who is:

respectful
self-respecting
intelligent
open-minded
accepting of my children
nonjudgmental
able to be silly at times
able to laugh—I want lots of laughter

not interested in care taking or being taken care of
willing to give me space
supportive of me making my own decisions
interested in travel
able to enjoy spending time with other people, not only me.

Your Turn to Write: "What I Want in a Relationship"

What do you want from a relationship? You may find it helpful, as Alicia did, to write down what you don't want as well as what you do want. What was missing from your last relationship? Respect? Companionship? Having fun together? Positive interactions with your children? What criteria do you have for a man with whom you might get involved? That he has a steady job as well as a sense of humor? That he doesn't pressure you for sex on the first date? That he is family-oriented and makes spending time with family members a priority?

When you meet someone who interests you, keep your criteria in mind as you get to know him. How well does he fit your needs? Are there any warning signs that he may meet the criteria on your checklist for characteristics you don't want? Go slowly in the beginning of the relationship to give yourself the time you need to evaluate what you are getting from the relationship.

Section II

Focusing on Yourself

24 *"What I Want for Myself"*

When was the last time you sat down and really thought about what *you* want for *yourself*? Not what someone else wants for you. Not what you want for someone else. What you want for you.

If it's been a long time since you did this, or you've never done this at all, today's a good time to start.

Society tells women that they should place the needs of others before their own. The traditional image of a "good" woman is one who makes sacrifices for her family. But what about your own needs? It's not healthy to continually attend to the needs of others while ignoring your own. Finding a balance between meeting the needs of others (for example, your children's) and meeting your own is a key to a happier, more satisfying life.

But perhaps you're not even sure what your needs are. The first step you must take is to begin figuring out what you want for yourself. Maggie wrote on this topic not long after leaving Russell:

I want solitude, peace, relaxation. These past few months haven't given me these things and I crave them. The days and months go on, dealing with courts, lawyers and my children. All the demands, the stress and fighting for my children and myself to have our rights respected. I find little time for the things I crave.

Every day is like being in a war that never seems to stop. I am trying my hardest to get what I need, but it's difficult with so much going on and all the negativity I have to deal with.

I hope I win this war because I am looking forward to the day when I am strong enough to get what I want for myself, which is a full education and a strong bond with my children that cannot be broken.

Your Turn to Write: "What I Want for Myself"

Think about what you want for yourself. Just let your thoughts flow. Start writing. Write without stopping or pausing. If you get stuck, keep writing, "I want, I want, I want. . ." until something comes out. Try to let things bubble up from beneath your conscious mind and out onto the page.

25 Remembering and Reclaiming Childhood Goals

Think back to when you were a young girl and the world was full of wonderful possibilities. You saw animals, faces and castles in the shapes of clouds drifting overhead as you lay in the tickly grass. You read books that took you to other lands, let you ride bareback on a chestnut stallion, solve mysteries and be scared by ghosts. You had a favorite doll or stuffed animal which you talked to and which you were convinced was alive.

You dreamed imaginative dreams, both awake and asleep. You felt you could do anything or be anybody. You believed you could fulfill your heart's desire.

What happened to that ability to dream?

Women who are in abusive relationships often are so occupied with day-to-day safety and survival that they do not have time to dream. Thoughts of a positive future start to slip away as they begin feeling depressed and hopeless.

It's difficult to have the time, energy and clarity to dream about what you'd like to do—go back to school, make new friends, get a different job—if you're forever worrying whether he'll think the house isn't clean enough or if you'll be able to keep the kids quiet during dinner so that he won't explode.

Now that you're on your own, there are still lots of responsibilities that occupy you, perhaps so many that you still sometimes feel overwhelmed. But you are resourceful. You must be or you wouldn't have gotten out of that relationship and to the point you're at now. Now that you're away from the daily stress of living with an abusive partner, away from the yelling, the belittling, the nitpicking and the accusing, away from the fear of being hit if you don't do everything exactly as he wants, you're free to start remembering and reclaiming the dreams you once had.

It's been so long. How do you start?

One way is to remember back to when you were a child. What did you envision yourself doing when you grew up? Did you want to be a dancer, a lawyer, a mother, a computer operator, a veterinarian, a writer, a business owner, a wife, a day care operator, a landscaper, an artist, a scientist, a teacher, a police officer, a long distance trucker? Begin with these first dreams. Remember how it made you feel to imagine yourself living these dreams? As young children, we firmly believe that we can be and do whatever we want. Remember that feeling of confidence, the thrill of endless possibility?

Anna recalled that she always wanted to be one of the women behind the cosmetics counter at a big department store because they always seemed so poised and confident. She used to imagine herself beautifully dressed and with an elegant hairstyle making sale after sale to satisfied customers. When she remembered that childhood fantasy, she realized that accomplishing it was entirely possible and decided to look into a career in sales.

Your Turn to Write: Remembering and Reclaiming Childhood Goals

If you have a photograph of yourself as a child, study it and remember what you dreamed about doing when you grew up. If you have had to leave all of your possessions behind when you broke free from your abuser and no longer have childhood photos, do the same exercise by picturing your young self in your mind's eye. Take a moment to recall the feelings of confidence and possibility that you had as a little girl when you imagined your future.

Now, write on the topic "What I Wanted to Be When I Grew Up." You may choose to write in a child's voice, as if you were that age again. You may try writing about your childhood goals at different ages. For instance:

When I was five I wanted to be a doctor because when I went to the doctor's office she always let me listen to my heartbeat with her stethoscope. I thought that if I became a doctor I could do that all the time. When I was nine I wanted to be a horse trainer; I planned to live in a room above the stable and ride horses all day. When I was thirteen I wanted to be a veterinarian because I loved animals. When I was sixteen I wanted to be a wife and mother and make a beautiful home for my family.

Are you identifying any goals from your childhood that

you still would like to fulfill today? Perhaps you are realizing that you always wanted to work with animals, be a teacher, run a restaurant, have children. What can you do to fulfill those childhood dreams now?

26 "I'm Most Proud Of. . ."

You have accomplished so much since getting away from your ex-partner—found a new place to live, navigated the legal system, took care of your kids during the difficult transition. Have you taken the time to pat yourself on the back?

It is possible that, in the midst of upheaval and change, all the various details of the work you've done as you establish a safe, healthy life for yourself and your kids have blurred together. You may have forgetten to take a step back and give yourself credit for your accomplishments. It is especially powerful for women who have been abused to do this since often their partners told them they were not capable of doing *anything*.

Maggie wrote about her proudest achievement:

The most rewarding accomplishment is being a role model for my children, showing that I can break patterns and change the odds on being a winner against mental and physical abuse.

Your Turn to Write: "I'm Most Proud Of. . . "

Write down all that you can remember having accomplished since being on your own. This list may include any positive step, from finding a nice apartment to having a closer relationship with your children to learning how to manage on a tight budget. Maybe you have taken a computer class or learned how to swim. Maybe you've gained more insight into yourself. Maybe you stopped smoking or biting your nails.

Circle the three achievements for which you feel proudest. From these three, choose the one accomplishment most important to you. Once you've made your selection, write about that accomplishment. How did you approach doing it? What kept you from accomplishing it in the past and what's different in your life now that you were able to do it? Once you made up your mind to do it, was it difficult or easy? How did you feel when you did it? How do you feel about it now?

27 "Making My Own Choices"

When you were with your abusive partner, did he allow you to make choices? Perhaps he did, but were you "punished" if you made the wrong choice? When an abuser puts you in this type of no-win situation, you can be made to feel helpless about your ability to make choices and maintain control over your life.

You may also have felt helpless if your ex made all the decisions, big and small, and didn't allow you to have any choices at all. Perhaps he decided when you should get up in the morning, whether or not you could take a shower, what clothes you could or could not wear, what you could or could not do during the day, who you could or could not talk to, what you would make for dinner, what the two of you would watch on television (and how late and how loud), when you could go to bed. You felt as if you were in prison. You had to follow your ex's rules or you paid the consequences. You learned that challenging him resulted in his hurting or humiliating you, so you went along with his decisions. After a while, the idea of making your own choices and decisions became so foreign to you that you weren't sure you knew how anymore.

But while this was happening—because of it and in spite of it—you made one of the hardest and most courageous choices of your life: you chose to leave him.

Now you have the freedom to make your own choices again, large and small. Many women who have been abused by their partners say that being able to make small choices, such as what to make for dinner, when to watch TV and when to go to bed, are initially the most gratifying. Day-to-day decision-making comprises the rhythm and quality of your life. Graciela illustrated the importance of being able to make her own everyday choices in this piece:

It's nice to be able to make my own decisions again, free of the dictator and his oppressive rules. I feel exhilarated thinking about all the choices and possibilities I have now that he's out of my life. I have the choice of what foods to cook, and since being away from him I've made my favorite meals every night.

I'm determined to make the best choices for Carmen and myself. Hector wouldn't let me get Carmen any pets and now we have a puppy. I could rarely have friends over before, but now I have them over for coffee or dinner.

It seems I'm making new decisions and choices now on a daily basis, and it feels great. But I think the best choice I have made so far was leaving him.

. . .

Your Turn to Write: "Making My Own Choices"

What choices are you able to make now that you weren't allowed to make before? How does it feel to have the freedom to make these choices? Is it difficult, easy, fun, frightening? What have been some of the hardest choices you have been faced with, and how did you deal with them? What choices have you found the most fun to make?

Think about what criteria you use when making choices and decisions. Do you think about how the choice you make will help you reach your long-term goals? Do you consider each choice or decision in regard to your mental and physical health, your safety and peace of mind? Is your choice a satisfying one? How so, and what about it is satisfying? Might your choice jeopardize your safety or health in any way?

Be conscious of the choices you make. This will help keep your choices positive and beneficial for you.

28 Finding Support and Making New Friends

In Part I, we talked about people who came through for you when you needed them, and people who disappointed you when you turned to them for help. Hopefully, this discussion helped you unravel the healthy from the unhealthy parts of your support system. This process is an important part of establishing an emotionally (and physically) safe life for yourself. If people who supposedly care about you are putting you down or making you feel that you can't accomplish something rather than being supportive of your efforts, you are leaving yourself emotionally vulnerable if you choose to associate with them.

You deserve to have supportive, healthy people in your life, people who will not chastize or criticize you. You do not need to hear, "I told you so" or "Well, what did you expect? You always choose guys like that." Healthy, supportive people contribute positively to your feeling of safety and your ability to grow. Unhealthy, nonsupportive people detract from them.

Sometimes, though, staying away from unhealthy, negative or inappropriate people is a lot more difficult than it sounds. Like your ex, these people may have a good side, too. Maybe they're fun to be with, such as the girlfriend who calls and invites you to go out dancing. Sure, you figure, why not, we'll have a lot of laughs. But when she leaves you stranded because she's gone home with a guy she met at the club, she's put you in a difficult and possibly unsafe situation.

Anna is working to distinguish healthy from unhealthy supports:

I still want to pick up the phone and call him. I can't believe I still want to talk to him. Sometimes I think, "I could just call him to see what he's thinking or doing. It wouldn't mean anything. We had some great times together, remember. And he can be so much fun to talk to."

Then I stop myself. Wait a minute. Remember, this is the guy who isolated you from your friends. He's the one who slept with another woman and gave you a sexually transmitted disease that cost $600 in medical bills to fix. On top of it all, he denied the whole affair.

I still have to stop and run the laundry list through my mind to stop myself from calling him. Running through the list is the best way I've found to keep myself safe and happy. I must forget about him. It's crucial for me and my children that I stay healthy.

Sometimes I feel so very lonely. That's when I want to call him. So then I know it's important for me to call someone else, like a close friend from my support group. I know that she will understand how I'm feeling because she's a single mom in the same position, who feels the same way about the man who was

in her life. We can joke about our loneliness and share our rage. We can tell each other about our kids' activities and our dreams for improving our lives. I tell her she can do it, she can achieve her dreams. She gives me some realistic suggestions to make my dreams happen.

Bill would never have told me how to achieve my dreams. That's another reason not to call him.

Anna recognizes that she gets the urge to call her ex-partner when she's feeling "so very lonely." In her written piece, she has identified when she feels most vulnerable to slipping back into old, unhealthy patterns. In order to combat this danger, she has devised a method to remind herself why calling him is not ultimately in her best interests.

But Anna goes beyond that. In addition to running her "laundry list," Anna then calls someone who she knows will truly be supportive of her. In this case, Anna calls another woman she knows shares many of her life experiences, a woman who knows what Anna is going through and who will not be judgmental of her.

Your Turn to Write: Finding Support and Making New Friends

Think about all the different people in your life. Which ones do you turn to for support? Think about the people in that group in terms of what this chapter is about. Which of these people fall into the healthy portion of your support system? What is it about them that made you categorize them as healthy supports?

Which people fall into the unhealthy part of your support system? What about them made you define them as unhealthy?

29 *"What Success Means to Me"*

In our society, success is often equated with material gain. Every time we read a magazine or watch television, we hear that we would be happier if we lived in a mansion, wore designer clothes, ate caviar and drank champagne. Women also get the message that to be successful you must have a man and be a perfect wife and mother, as well as earn a paycheck and look like a model.

When Alicia was still married to Jeff, she had all the material comfort she wanted: a spacious house in a quiet neighborhood, beautiful antique furniture, family vacations to Florida and the Bahamas. But Alicia was willing to give up that lifestyle in order to have a life free from Jeff's abuse. She says that, to her, success is knowing she can make it on her own, and that she doesn't have to be dependent on anyone.

Like Alicia, and thousands of other women who have left

abusive partners, you may have had to adjust to a different standard of material living—does this mean you are not successful? Quite the contrary. Anna shared how when one of her relatives called her new apartment a "closet," she laughed it off, saying, "To my way of thinking, the apartment was a palace; it represented a huge success because it meant I had gotten away from Bill."

Sometimes, though, it's hard to shake old ideas of success, even when we don't really believe in them anymore. But you have made a new beginning and you are in an excellent position to think about what success means to *you*. Once you have defined what success is, you can identify the steps to achieve it.

Your Turn to Write: "What Success Means to Me"

How do you sort out your definition of success from the meanings you are bombarded with every day? Try asking yourself questions such as, "Did I want to be a doctor or did my father want me to be a doctor?" "Do I really believe that I'm a failure because I couldn't keep my family together, or is that a measure of success my church wants me to embrace?" "Where am I getting the messages that I have to have a perfect body in order to be successful—from magazines, friends, my ex-partner? Do I really believe that?"

Based upon what you have discovered from completing the above process, what does success mean to *you*? What is it that you find meaningful in life: having a job that is rewarding both financially *and* emotionally? Challenging yourself to grow on an ongoing basis? Not being afraid to try new things and take calculated risks? Spending more time with your children? Finding a balance between home, job, friends and yourself? Choosing safety over abuse? Fulfilling your potential and encouraging your children to fulfill theirs?

In the next chapter you will use your definition of success to help you set and achieve goals.

30 *Setting Goals—and Achieving Them*

You may not realize that you already have experience in setting goals for yourself—and achieving them. But look at what you've accomplished: when you were trying to get out, your goal was to leave your abusive partner, and you achieved this! Perhaps your next goal was finding a new place to live, and the goal after that, putting a small amount of money aside each week so that you could buy winter coats or school supplies for the kids.

As you may have discovered, it's helpful to identify the specific steps you need to take in order to achieve each goal. Breaking the process down into small, doable steps makes the task less overwhelming. Also, as you achieve each step, you get a shot of positive reinforcement which encourages you to stick it out until you reach your goal.

So now you're on your own. What are your new goals? If you haven't yet thought about establishing goals for your new life, now is the time. Goals are important because they give our lives structure and purpose and keep us from simply drifting along. If you've been feeling stuck—whether because you hate your job but can't figure out how to quit, or because your new relationship is unsatisfying but you don't know how to break it off—setting goals is a great way to get yourself moving again.

Your Turn to Write: Setting Goals—and Achieving Them

For this exercise, start by focusing on relatively short-term goals, to make them more manageable. First, think about where you'd like to be one year from now, remembering to use the definition of success that you came up with in the last chapter to guide you. Write a list with as many one-year goals as you can think of. It may look something like this:

By the end of this year, I'd like to:

- Be in a GED or college program;
- Have joined a support group for women who have been abused;
- Have joined a book discussion group;
- Have taken a parenting class to learn more about being an effective parent;
- Have established a regular exercise routine;
- Have a garden;
- Visit my sister in South Carolina;
- Learn how to cook Mexican food.

Now, choose three of these goals to work toward for the next 365 days. Try to choose goals that are reachable within the time period. Choose at least one "practical goal" (return to school) and one "fun" goal (learn Mexican cooking). The third is up to you.

Divide your paper into two columns. In the left-hand column, write your three goals, leaving lots of space between them. In the right-hand column, write down how you're going to achieve each goal. Make your method as specific as possible—if you're vague about how you're going to work toward your goal, you'll soon get lost. You may want to write down the detailed steps you'll need to take. The first entry on your paper will look something like this:

Goals	*Steps*
Be in a GED or college program	• Go to library and find out what programs are available in my area. • Call the programs and ask them to send information. • Read through the information and identify what programs interest me. • Make a checklist of everything I need to do to apply (check for application deadlines). • Call the schools to find out about financial aid and make a checklist of what I

need to do to apply for assistance.

• Follow through on both my checklists.

• Look into potential transportation and child care arrangements.

Plan on measuring your progress on a monthly basis. Choose a day that has significance for you (for instance, if your birthday is May 14, choose the fourteenth of every month) to review your progress toward your goals. On that day, sit down with your goal list and note if you have or have not made progress, or if you have fully achieved the goal. This is also the time to decide whether to revise or discontinue any goals that are not currently feasible, or to re-evaluate how much time you need to accomplish a goal. Don't be judgmental with yourself. Part of this process is to learn how to devise realistic ways of achieving your goals, so if something doesn't work out the way you originally planned, use the revision as a learning experience.

31 Taking Care: Eating, Exercising, Relaxing

How do you take care of yourself?

If you have a hard time answering this question, you're not alone. Many women are excellent caretakers—of everyone but themselves! Many women have been taught that tending to their own needs is selfish; some women feel they don't deserve to nurture themselves. But if you don't take care of yourself, you'll end up depleted and exhausted, perhaps even depressed or perpetually angry.

Taking care of yourself can take many forms—you don't need to spend money to do it! Taking care of yourself means paying attention to the needs of your mind, body and spirit. It means eating healthy foods—whole grains, fruits and vegetables and less caffeine, sugar and fat. It means getting some exercise on a regular basis such as walking, swimming, dancing to the radio, learning yoga or aerobic dancing (if your library doesn't have a book or videotape on the exercise of your choice, ask if they can get one for you). Scientific research studies show that even a small amount of regular exercise can elevate your mood, keep you healthier and help you live longer.

Taking care also means finding the time to relax. This may mean fifteen minutes of quiet time with a cup of herbal tea, or doing some deep breathing and creative visualization as described in the next chapter. Write in your journal, read a book. Maggie says she takes ten minutes every morning before going to work to sit quietly in the kitchen, gazing out the window and thinking about nothing at all.

Taking care also means nourishing your spirit—laughing, playing, enjoying your children, family and friends. Spend time in nature: in the woods, on the beach, in the park. Alicia has a special apple orchard she drives by at least once a week so that she can enjoy looking at the trees. Spend quiet time alone; contemplate who you really are.

The important message here is for you to *take some time for yourself.*

Your Turn to Write: Taking Care: Eating, Exercising, Relaxing

Divide your paper into two columns. On the left-hand side, write down all the deterrents to taking care of yourself ("I don't have time"; "I don't deserve it"; "After I finish taking care of the kids, my job and the house, I don't have the energy.")

In the right-hand column, write down all the reasons

why you *should* take care of yourself ("I deserve it"; "It will make me a more generous person"; "It will make me feel better about myself"; "It will give me more energy.") How can you use the entries on the right-hand side of the paper to cancel out the entries on the left?

On a separate sheet of paper, write down all the ways you can think of to take care of yourelf. Include all aspects of your body, mind and spirit. Some suggestions for your list are:

- Find something to laugh about every day;
- Ride my bike to work instead of taking the bus;
- Learn how to meditate;
- Borrow some low-fat cookbooks from the library and learn how to prepare delicious, healthy meals;
- Spend time with my women friends—laughing, talking, dancing!
- Become more connected with nature: take hikes, go to the park, start a garden, get a houseplant;
- Throw out all the junk food in the house;
- Write about my thoughts and feelings in a journal;
- Cut down on coffee; quit smoking.

Choose an item from your list to do every day. Add to your list anytime you want.

32 Meditation and Creative Visualization

You have done an incredible job letting go of your ex-partner and establishing your new life. Take a moment to savor your accomplishment. Be very proud of yourself!

Your journey has not been easy, but you have overcome numerous obstacles and made significant strides. The most wonderful part of this journey is that it is ongoing. You can continue to grow and change and learn about yourself. You can continue setting and achieving goals. You can continue reaching for your dreams. It is a magnificent, lifelong process.

You can make it happen!

Your Turn to Write: Meditation and Creative Visualization

Sit comfortably in a chair or cross-legged on the floor. Close your eyes. Slowly take in a deep breath to the count of five. Hold the breath for five more counts. Slowly exhale, again to the count of five. When you breathe in, pull the air down to your abdomen. Your stomach should expand as you inhale and contract as you exhale.

Repeat this exercise ten times. Stay focused on your breathing. If your mind starts to wander, gently bring it back. Feel your body growing relaxed.

When you feel calm, form a picture of yourself in the life you want: surrounded by people who care about you; in a comfortable home; furthering your education; having your own business. Picture yourself accomplishing your dreams, using as much detail as possible. Picture yourself safe, healthy, content. Feel strong and confident.

Take two more deep breaths and slowly open your eyes.

In detail, write down what you saw in your visualization. What was it like, how did it feel, who was with you?

Use this meditation and visualization exercise on a regular basis. It will help you accomplish the safe, fulfilling life you want, and *deserve*.

Suggested Resources and Reading

National Domestic Violence Hotline

Spanish and English: 1.800.799.SAFE
TDD: 1.800.787-3224
Accessible 24-hours a day, seven days a week

Crisis intervention, information and referral. The Hotline uses up-to-date information on nationwide domestic violence shelters, legal advocacy and other assistance programs to connect callers to services in their area. Offers written material in a variety of languages and formats, and phone access to translators in 139 languages.

Books

Brady, Maureen. *Beyond Survival: A Writing Journey for Healing Childhood Sexual Abuse*. New York: Hazelden/HarperCollins, 1992.

Goldberg, Natalie. *Writing Down the Bones: Freeing the Writer Within*. Boston: Shambhala, 1986.

Goldberg, Natalie. *Wild Mind: Living the Writer's Life*. New York: Bantam, 1990.

Jones, Ann and Susan Schechter. *When Love Goes Wrong: What to Do When You Can't Do Anything Right—Strategies for Women with Controlling Partners*. New York: HarperCollins, 1992.

NiCarthy, Ginny. *Getting Free: You Can End Abuse and Take Back Your Life*. Seattle: Seal Press, 1982, 1986.

NiCarthy, Ginny. *The Ones Who Got Away: Women Who Left Abusive Partners*. Seattle: Seal Press, 1987.

About the Author

Sharon Doane, M.S.W., M.F.A., is the former program director for a county-wide domestic violence prevention program in New York. She has taught creative writing workshops for several years and has helped women use writing as part of their process of healing from abusive relationships.

Selected Titles from Seal Press

IN LOVE AND IN DANGER: *A Teen's Guide to Breaking Free of Abusive Relationships* by Barrie Levy. $8.95, 1-878067-26-5.

DATING VIOLENCE: *Young Women in Danger* edited by Barrie Levy. $16.95. 1-878067-03-6.

GETTING FREE: *You Can End Abuse and Take Back Your Life* by Ginny NiCarthy. $12.95, 0-931188-37-7. The most important self-help resource book of the domestic violence movement. Audiocassette: GETTING FREE: *Are You Abused? (And What to Do About It)* narrated by Ginny NiCarthy. 60 minutes. $10.95, 0-931188-84-9

You Can Be Free: An Easy-to-Read Handbook for Abused Women by Ginny NiCarthy and Sue Davidson. $6.95, 0-931188-68-7.

THE ONES WHO GOT AWAY: *Women Who Left Abusive Partners* by Ginny NiCarthy. $11.95, 0-931188-49-0.

A COMMUNITY SECRET: *For the Filipina in an Abusive Relationship* by Jacqueline Agtuca, in collaboration with The Asian Women's Shelter. $5.95, 1-878067-44-3. Written in easy-to-read English.

CHAIN CHAIN CHANGE: *For Black Women in Abusive Relationships*, expanded second edition, by Evelyn C. White. $8.95, 1-878067-60-5.

MEJOR SOLA QUE MAL ACOMPAÑADA: *For the Latina in an Abusive Relationship/Para la Mujer Golpeada* by Myrna M. Zambrano. $10.95, 0-931188-26-1. A bilingual handbook in Spanish and English.

MOMMY AND DADDY ARE FIGHTING: *A Book for Children About Family Violence* by Susan Paris. $8.95, 0-931188-33-4. Illustrated by Gail Labinski.

NAMING THE VIOLENCE: *Speaking Out Against Lesbian Battering*, edited by Kerry Lobel. $12.95, 0-931188-42-3.

THE SINGLE MOTHER'S COMPANION: *Essays and Stories by Women*, edited by Marsha R. Leslie. $12.95, 1-878067-56-7.

THE BLACK WOMAN'S HEALTH BOOK: *Speaking for Ourselves*, edited by Evelyn C. White. $16.95, 1-878067-40-0.

THE LESBIAN PARENTING BOOK: *A Guide to Creating Families and Raising Children* by D. Merilee Clunis and G. Dorsey Green. $16.95, 1-878067-68-0.